Claudia Curi · Maurizio Murgia

Bank CEOs

Characteristics, Compensation Policies, and Impacts on Bank Performance

Springer

Claudia Curi
Faculty of Economics and Management
Free University of Bozen-Bolzano
Bolzano
Italy

Maurizio Murgia
Faculty of Economics and Management
Free University of Bozen-Bolzano
Bolzano
Italy

ISSN 2193-1720 ISSN 2193-1739 (electronic)
SpringerBriefs in Finance
ISBN 978-3-319-90865-6 ISBN 978-3-319-90866-3 (eBook)
https://doi.org/10.1007/978-3-319-90866-3

Library of Congress Control Number: 2018940883

Printed on acid-free paper

This Springer imprint is published by the registered company Springer International Publishing AG part of Springer Nature
The registered company address is: Gewerbestrasse 11, 6330 Cham, Switzerland

SpringerBriefs in Finance

More information about this series at http://www.springer.com/series/10282

Contents

1 Introduction 1
1.1 Setting the Boundaries of the Book: Why Do CEOs Matter to the Banking Industry? 1
1.2 Book Outline and Objectives of Each Chapter 3
References 5

2 Banks Are Special: Are Bank CEOs Alike? 7
2.1 The Financial Industry and the Labour Market for Executives 7
2.2 Bank CEO Incentives and the Role of Regulation 13
2.3 Determinants of Bank CEO Compensation 18
References 22

3 Theory and Stylised Facts of Bank CEO Pay Consequences 27
3.1 CEO Characteristics and Performance Consequences 27
3.2 CEO Compensation, Risk-Taking and Performance 31
3.3 CEO Compensation and Corporate Policies 38
References 40

4 Characteristics and Pay Packages of CEOs at the Largest European Banks: Some Empirical Evidence 45
4.1 Introduction 45
4.2 Data, Sample Selection Criteria, and Variable Construction 47
4.3 Results and Discussion 50
References 54

5 Conclusions 55

Chapter 1
Introduction

Abstract In this chapter, we set the boundaries of the book, highlighting why CEOs have been important to the banking industry in the past and will continue to be important in the near future. We conclude in this chapter with a description of the book's outline and the objectives of each chapter.

1.1 Setting the Boundaries of the Book: Why Do CEOs Matter to the Banking Industry?

The 2008–2009 financial crisis threatened the global financial system with total collapse, leading to the bailouts of many large financial institutions, a slump in stock prices, and declines in consumer lending and investments in the real sector. New financial regulatory reforms, such as the *Dodd-Frank Act*, *Basel III*, and stress tests, were introduced with the aim of increasing financial institutions' compliance obligations and, consequently, the stability of the financial system. However, the financial crisis paved the way for the rise of the Fintech sector, which proposed a culture of efficient operational design, innovations for the provision of specific services, low-leverage solutions, and mostly equity-financed business models. Such concepts contrast with the basic pillars of today's banking industry. These changes prompted regulatory reform and technological innovation in the financial services sector, which opened the door to a new era in banking, challenged the existing organisation of the industry, and blurred the boundaries of the financial sector. In the near future, the banking industry has been called on to facilitate strategic disintermediation, revolutionise how incumbents create and deliver products and services, provide new gateways for entrepreneurship, democratise access to financial services (Philippon 2017), adopt new technological tools (such as cryptocurrencies and the blockchain, new digital advisory and trading systems, artificial intelligence and machine learning, peer-to-peer lending, equity crowdfunding and mobile payment systems) and comply with stricter rules, particularly for the industry giants—Global Systemically Important Banks (G-SIBs).

An important aspect of these new regulatory and technology trends is that the transformation of banking will be initiated and mostly driven by CEOs, who in turn

C. Curi and M. Murgia, *Bank CEOs*, SpringerBriefs in Finance,
https://doi.org/10.1007/978-3-319-90866-3_1

will personally mandate the choice of top management. It follows that bank CEOs will play a crucial role in shaping the future of the banking sector. Bank CEOs must play a special role in the forthcoming restructuring of the industry, tuning into the special role that banks have in the economic system. Thus, as banks are already recognised to be "special firms" due to their high leverage, asset opaqueness, business complexity and a highly skilled workforce (Philippon and Reshef 2012), CEOs must become the main drivers of bank transformation. However, looking to past years' events in the financial industry, we observe that bank CEOs have been in the spotlight. They have attracted scrutiny and overwhelmingly negative attention for their shamefully-high pay levels, which are often considered to have contributed to the recent financial crisis. In this regard, regulatory authorities have directly intervened to influence CEO pay structures with the aim of curbing the risk-taking behaviour and spiralling compensation levels that could affect the real economy.

As significant transformations are forthcoming in the banking industry, it is timely to take stock of how CEOs have influenced the performance, risk-taking behaviour and stability of banks through their personal and professional "style". In this book, we address the following question: When a powerful CEO is considering a sizable investment plan, complex financing in capital markets or similar strategic decisions, is he/she able to imprint his/her personal mark on those strategic directions? The literature has already indicated that some CEOs' characteristics are correlated with measures of firm performance and risk. We also know that CEOs' personal or "innate" characteristics have different influences on performance and risk than the "acquired" characteristics gained through professional experience and networking. Moreover, bank CEOs' business decisions may differ from value-maximising objectives, either because of agency conflicts inside the firm or because CEOs suffer from systematic cognitive biases or limitations that lead them to make, despite their best intentions, the wrong choices for shareholders.

The remuneration given to bank CEOs is the other factor that can interact with CEO characteristics and external mechanisms to affect banking performance. Such external mechanisms are often dictated by regulation (for instance, bonus caps), corporate governance (for instance, "say on pay" and turnover), corporate investment decisions (for instance, important restructuring programs), and bank leverage structures. These entangled relationships raise serious concerns about how the risk-taking incentives provided to CEOs impact business policies and the extent of the various risks banks typically face, which can be detrimental to financial health and, ultimately, to the survival of banking firms. None of the existing theories and growing body of empirical evidence on this issue are fully convincing, such that a debate is now emerging in the field.

A clear understating of these mechanisms will shed light on future issues and new research areas. Moreover, an assessment of the "state of the art" on bank CEO topics will provide useful information for unexplored research areas. While the literature on CEOs of nonfinancial firms is extensive and has established some important conclusions, the literature on bank CEOs is much scarcer and its findings are sometimes contradictory. Furthermore, as in many fields of economics and finance, most empirical studies have analysed US banks and their managers. European banks and, especially, the CEOs of European financial institutions, have rarely appeared in published research. This bias toward US banks is frequently explained by a lack of independent data or to less frequent disclosure of CEO compensation structures by European banks. In this book, we make an effort to breach this area of inquiry and make the first attempt to empirically examine the relationships between CEO characteristics, compensation structures, and the performance and risk of the very largest European banks (financial conglomerates). If bank CEOs are special, CEOs at the helm of these banks are even more so ("superstars"), given the influence they have on the financial stability of their firms and the entire economy.

This book first provides several reviews that provide valuable perspectives on the topic of bank CEOs that are well represented in published research papers. Secondly, on each topic, we not only provide a review of the existing research, but also indicate directions for future research.

We believe that this book takes a useful step in exploring links between bank CEO characteristics, compensation policies, and metrics of bank performance and risk. Such links have been widely discussed but have received scarce research attention, particularly in relation to European banks. Fruitful directions for future research may include exploration of the major and unsolved issues related to the distortion caused by provision of risk-taking incentives to CEOs. In fact, if CEOs were held responsible for the financial crisis, the future of the banking industry and its future transformation would be in their hands. While the means of producing and distributing financial products and services might change with technology innovation, the powerful influences of CEO job markets and agency conflicts will remain important, or may even increase. The writing style makes the chapters accessible to industry practitioners. For Ph.D. students and academics, the surveys offer dense roadmaps into the empirical research landscape and provide suggestions for future work.

Lastly, we would like to acknowledge financial support from the Faculty of Economics and Management of the Free University of Bolzano-Bozen, Italy, and the editorial support provided by Maria Cristina Acocella, Associate Editor of SpringerBriefs in Finance.

1.2 Book Outline and Objectives of Each Chapter

This book is structured in five chapters. The first establishes why the analysis of the role of CEOs in the banking industry is important. In the second, we analyse the connections between the bank CEO labour market, contractual incentives, and compensation schemes. More specifically, the goal of Chap. 2 is to address the following questions. What are the characteristics that distinguish the banking CEO labour market from other CEO labour markets in the financial sector? How has this market evolved, particularly after the 2008 financial crisis and the subsequent regulation of CEO and bank manager pay structures? We discuss answers to these questions, highlighting similarities and differences between the financial and nonfinancial sectors. We identify the causes and mechanisms of the strikingly high compensation levels that have been observed since the mid-1980s, focusing on topics related to the peculiarities of compensation for bank CEOs. As banks are considered "special firms" in an economic system, we argue that banking CEOs are all alike. We then discuss the impacts of regulatory mechanisms on CEO pay schemes and the typical agency problems that arise. Conflicts between CEOs and providers of external financing (e.g. shareholders and debtholders) happen frequently due to the distorted incentives embedded into CEO compensation contracts. This was particularly evident in the lead-up to the 2008 financial crisis. We review the main regulatory interventions implemented in the US and EU after the financial crisis in response to this issue. We conclude Chap. 2 with a description of the interconnected factors that may affect bank executive incentives.

In Chap. 3, we discuss the available empirical evidence on the impact of bank CEO compensation on several firm-level outcomes, such as bank performance and strategic decisions. We also discuss the relationship between CEO turnover and how compensation policies changed in the years encompassing the financial crisis. More specifically, if bank CEOs are special, as each bank is, do banks' business characteristics influence the ways that CEOs make complex and non-routine strategic decisions? Do CEOs leave their mark or have a personal style when making investment, financing and other strategic decisions? Moreover, how do the incentives for risk-taking that are implicit in CEO remuneration contracts interact with unobservable CEO characteristics? Chapter 3 also reviews the major research in the field, highlighting how different CEO characteristics (personal and acquired) contribute to performance and risk-taking. We present empirical evidence of the sensitivity of CEO pay to bank performance and risk in pre-crisis years, and the role it played in causing the recent financial crisis. We discuss contrasting findings, highlighting the debated relationship between pre-crisis CEO incentives to bear higher risks and crisis-period bank performance. We then discuss the main regulatory interventions undertaken in response to this issue and their suitability in light of recent banking CEO compensation models. We conclude Chap. 3 with a description of CEO incentives in relation to strategic decisions, such as mergers and acquisitions and restructuring programs, and how these may influence bank performance and risk.

In Chap. 4, we present some new empirical evidence based on a current database of the traits of CEOs operating in the largest European banks. Do the personal and professional characteristics of CEOs play a role in the performance and risk-exposure of the largest European financial conglomerates? Are their compensation structures alike? In this chapter, we empirically test these relationships, highlighting the main differences with the results reported in the literature and addressing future research directions. We present descriptive statistics of our sample of financial conglomerates and related CEOs before presenting our empirical evidence. We construct two models: one where the dependent variable is Tobin's q, and the other where the dependent variable is the financial conglomerate risk. Since financial conglomerates have complex and diversified businesses, we construct the model from an income and asset diversity perspective. Our first analysis shows that CEO tenure and experience in the financial industry are factors that enhance the market value of financial conglomerates, although having an older CEO might be detrimental. Moreover, while bonuses have positive effects on performance, the fixed components of CEO remuneration are value-destroying. On the one hand, professional experience typically helps a CEO to achieve higher performance; on the other, it increases a bank's risk exposure. Tenure length, however, could act as a hedging mechanism. In Chap. 5, we discuss the main conclusions.

References

Philippon, T. 2017. The Fintech Opportunity. In *BIS Working Papers*: Bank For International Settlements.

Philippon, T., and A. Reshef. 2012. Wages and human capital in the US finance industry: 1909–2006. *Quarterly Journal of Economics* 127 (4): 1551–1609.

Chapter 2
Banks Are Special: Are Bank CEOs Alike?

Abstract What are the distinguishing characteristics of the CEO labour market in the financial sector? How has this market evolved, particularly after the 2008 financial crisis and the subsequent regulation of CEO and bank manager pay structures? In this chapter, we discuss answers to these questions, highlighting similarities and differences between the financial and nonfinancial industries. We identify the causes and mechanisms of the strikingly high compensation levels that have been observed since the mid-1980s, focusing on topics related to the peculiarities of compensation for bank CEOs. As banks are considered special firms in an economic system, we argue that banking CEOs are alike. We then discuss the impacts of regulatory mechanisms on CEO pay schemes and the agency problems that they can cause. Conflicts between CEOs and shareholders and debtholders arise from distorted incentives embedded into CEO compensation structures, which were particularly evident in the lead-up to the 2008 financial crisis. We review the main regulatory interventions implemented in the US and EU after the financial crisis. We conclude this chapter with a description of the interconnected factors that may affect bank executive incentives.

2.1 The Financial Industry and the Labour Market for Executives

The labour market in the financial services sector has recently attracted considerable interest among economists. One of the most striking features of the finance labour market is that, since the beginning of the 1980s, the average remuneration it provides has become greater and less evenly distributed across pay scales (more skewed) than in other economic sectors.

Oyer (2008) and Philippon and Reshef (2012) present compelling empirical evidence that the financial industry offers higher compensation than other sectors of the economy, even after controlling for individual characteristics and other exogenous factors. Bell and Van Reenen (2013) reported an average compensation of £1,905,000 among a sample of 1408 senior bankers in the United Kingdom in 2010, and Kaplan and Rauh (2009) show that a significant proportion of the highest US incomes stem from the financial sector. It is interesting to note that Kaplan and Rauh

C. Curi and M. Murgia, *Bank CEOs*, SpringerBriefs in Finance,
https://doi.org/10.1007/978-3-319-90866-3_2

argue that their evidence is consistent with theories of skill-biased technological change, superstar-type explanations and greater scale (and the interaction of these theories) than other proposed theories of work compensation. Further, their findings are in line with Oyer (2008) estimates that the lifetime net pay premium enjoyed by an MBA graduate working in financial services could be high as US$1.5–5 million relative to other sectors (such as consulting). Moreover, the financial sector pay premium has substantially risen during recent decades. However, this pay premium is not equally distributed across all finance industry subsectors. Higher average pay premiums have been primarily observed for employees and partners working in the investment banking, security trading and asset management businesses, whereas the average pay in the credit intermediation and insurance subsectors has not increased as much. It is worth noting that empirical studies report that the group of financial industry professionals who earn the highest rewards for their expertise are traders in over-the-counter (OTC) markets. For example, before the recent financial crisis, managing directors trading exotic credit derivatives earned, on average, $3.4 million per year. More recently, the average salaries paid to various types of OTC traders grew by 10% in 2014 alone.

Several studies have documented the high and rising nature of finance sector compensation and, in general, the evolution of the labour market for financial industry executives across different countries and institutional contexts. Philippon and Reshef (2012) were the first to deeply analyse the US financial industry. Subsequently, Boustanifar et al. (2017) extended the Philippon and Reshef (2012) approach to a sample of 23 developed countries. Using a different but complementary lens, Bell and Van Reenen (2013) and Lindley and McIntosh (2017) focused on the growing inequality at the top end of the wage distribution in the UK financial sector, while Célérier and Vallée (2015) studied the finance premium for the French financial sector. Philippon and Reshef (2012) paper is a trailblazer in this research area, as analysed the past century's evolution of average wages along with the evolution of education, the wages of top managers, human capital, and job complexity in the US financial services industry. They showed that, when graphed, data on wages in finance (relative to the non-farm private sector) produced a U-shaped curve between 1909 and 2006. By 2006, the average worker in finance earned 70% more than the average (non-finance) private sector worker. Workers in finance earned the same education-adjusted wages as other workers until 1990, but by 2006, the average wage premium increased by 50%. The pattern is the same for top earners but the differences are larger; the wages of top decile earners in finance grew 80% more than that of nonfinancial sector top decile earners. By 2005, finance executives earned 250% more than executives in non-financial industries. Not surprisingly, the work location influences average pay levels: workers in the Tri-State Area (New York, New Jersey and Connecticut) are able to earn a 300% premium. The same U-shaped pattern of wages data over time is exhibited by education level data for the financial sector. From 1909 to 1933, the financial sector was a high-wage industry, composed mainly of highly educated employees. The proportion of skilled workers in finance is 17% higher than in the general private sector, and these workers are, on average, paid 50% more than workers in other economic sectors. A dramatic change occurred after the Great Depression (mid-

1930s). The financial sector started losing its high-human capital and high-wage status. Most of the decline occurred during the 1950s, and it continued gradually until the early 1980s. By that time, relative wages in the finance sector were approximately equal to those in the rest of the economy. From the mid-1980s onward, another significant shift occurred. The financial sector became a high-skill/high-wage industry again. Philippon and Reshef (2012) show that changes in relative wages are driven by changes in the composition of education and, particularly, by the set of occupations within the finance sector. In contrast, changes inside finance subsectors, such as credit intermediation (by banks, savings institutions, and companies that provide credit services), insurance, and other finance industries (securities, commodities, venture capital, private equity, hedge funds, trusts, and other investment activities, including investment banks), are irrelevant. Changes in finance occupations are important in influencing relative wages, and the authors show that this phenomenon is linked to change in the complexity of tasks performed within the finance industry (i.e., routine manual tasks, routine cognitive tasks, analytical thinking tasks, nonroutine manual tasks). The analysis confirms that the relative complexity of jobs in the finance industry can be represented by a similar U-shape pattern as that of wages and education (relative to the nonfarm private sector). Within all three subsectors of finance, job complexity has changed over time and the sector lost much of its analytical complexity (i.e. requiring math aptitude) between 1910 and 1950. At that point, a slow recovery started and accelerated through the 1990s. Decision making (direction, control and planning) suffered even more in relative terms but the recovery has been much stronger. Routine task intensity increased in finance from 1910 to 1930 and started to decline from 1980 onwards. In all cases, the timing of these shifts suggests a distinct role for deregulation, which appears to be the most robust determinant of all these patterns. The authors documented significant effects of financial regulation on demand for human capital in finance. They found that when significant reductions in regulation occur, the financial sector increases the scope for skilled workers to operate freely and use their own creativity to produce new complex products. This intensifies the level of financial innovation and, at the same time, competition for talent in the job market. In contrast, tighter regulation is likely to lead to an outflow of human capital from the industry.

Boustanifar et al. (2017) expanded on the Philippon and Reshef (2012) study by examining a sample of 23 developed countries[1] over the 1970–2011 period. They found significant heterogeneity in the trends of relative finance wages across countries: twelve countries had increases, while the remaining eleven had either decreases or mixed trends. Moreover, in countries that had significant increases in relative finance wages, skilled workers accounted for more than the total increase. One exception was presented by Ibert et al. (2017) for mutual fund managers; while there is a strong relationship between the labour income of managers and the size of the funds under their management, the relationship is concave.

---

[1]The sample includes Australia, USA, Spain, Netherland, Norway, Denmark, Germany, Canada, Finland, Italy, Austria, Ireland, Sweden, South Korea, Portugal, Luxembourg, Czech Republic, Hungary, UK, Japan, France, Belgium and Sweden.

Bell and Van Reenen (2013) and Lindley and McIntosh (2017) analysed how high UK financial sector salaries are an important feature of the growing inequality that exists at the top end of the wage distribution. The first paper documents increasing 'extreme' wage inequality by focusing on the income growth of the top 1% of UK workers between 1998 and 2008. The increase is particularly extreme among bankers, even though they account for only one-third of the top percentile of the worker sample. Further, they found that 60% of the increase in this extreme wage inequality can be attributed to growth in bonuses. The paper by Lindley and McIntosh (2017) expanded this focus to the entire distribution of finance wages and reported that wage premiums are received by finance workers in all sub-sectors and occupations, and from all points of the wage distribution. By examining a sample of talented French engineers from 1983 to 2011, Célérier and Vallée (2015) confirmed these findings. They showed that talented French workers in the finance sector are better paid than talented workers in other industries. Finance premiums have increased threefold since the 1980s and grew 25% over the sample period consistent with results by Glode and Lowery (2016).

Although rising wages in the finance sector have been documented in several countries, the causes and mechanisms that give rise to this phenomenon are not entirely clear. Researchers have put forward several explanations. The first potential explanation is related to rent-sharing, whereby rents created in the finance sector are shared with employees. For example, Bivens and Mishel (2013), with reference to the US but also with relevance to the UK, suggest that the removal (or reduction) of regulations in the finance sector, the implicit insurance provided by government bail-outs of struggling financial institutions, and the increasing complexity of financial instruments that allow financial workers to hide risk from their investors, have all helped to create and increasingly extract rents in the finance sector. Bivens and Mishel (2013) also discuss an increasing incentive to do so in the form of falling marginal tax rates on high incomes, which increases the benefit of pursuing a larger share of rents. The second explanation is related to skill-biased technological change. The basic idea is that the falling price of information technology has led to the substitution of routine labour by technology capital. As routine tasks tend to be performed in jobs situated in the middle of the job quality distribution, economies with access to information technology have witnessed decreasing employment in the middle of the earnings distribution. Consequently, employment has become polarised into high- and low-paid jobs and inequality has risen. Here, routine tasks are thought to be substitutable with new technology, whilst high-skill, analytical, non-routine tasks are thought to be complementary to the technology. An analysis of skill intensity and task-use in the finance sector would determine the relevance of this theory in explaining the high and increasing nature of pay premiums in the sector. This conjecture contrasts with Philippon and Reshef (2012) results, which instead revealed that the pervasiveness of asymmetric information in finance leads to a different effect of regulations compared with other industries, where we expect wage reductions, not increases (as illustrated by Goodhart et al. (1998)). A tight link between deregulation and the flow of human capital in and out of the finance industry has been observed, and increasing regulation inhibits the creativity of skilled workers. In the wake of Depression-era regulations, highly skilled labour left the finance industry and returned precisely when these regulations were gradually removed in the 1980s and 1990s. This link holds for the entire finance industry and its sub-sectors, and has different effects compared to other industries.

In line with these results, Boustanifar et al. (2017) confirm that financial deregulation is the most important determinant of relative wages in finance for developed countries other than the US. However, the effect of deregulation is greatest in countries with financial systems that rely more on capital market finance and non-traditional banking (versus bank-oriented financial systems), and have a greater share of securitisation and trading in OTC markets. These findings are consistent with the view that greater regulation of financial systems limits the scope and scale of financial activity within the financial services sector; in particular, activities that are more prone to greater risk-taking and are likely associated with socially inefficient informational rents. All this is consistent with recent theories that stress the role of information asymmetry and complexity in giving rise to informational rents and excessive risk-taking in finance. See, for example, Korinek and Kreamer (2014) and Bolton et al. (2016).[2]

Boustanifar et al. (2017) also report that the impact of financial deregulation on workers' pay is greatest in countries with more flexible labour markets, and where the sector is less competitive. In fact, in the last few decades, the financial sector, particularly the investment banking business, has experienced increasing competition for managerial talent. As argued by Morrison and Wilhelm (2008), this development occurred primarily in investment banking, since the increased importance of economies of scale associated with new technologies made the partnership model obsolete and induced investment banks to become corporate entities and go public. While partnerships encourage close relationships between employees and pose a natural obstacle to their mobility, the greater transparency of corporations facilitates the poaching of star employees and decreases their corporate loyalty. This development also occurred in commercial banking, which once entailed a great deal of local knowledge and networking, so that over their careers, bank managers developed employer- and location-specific skills. This development brings a new geography to the banking sector that is much less local owing to the increasing role of large banks, the greater distances between banks and customers, and a reliance on hard rather than soft information in lending (see Petersen and Rajan 2002; Berger et al. 2005). This new scenario is characterised by an increase in managerial mobility even beyond the financial industry, as witnessed by the historical trend towards outside CEO appointments (Huson et al. 2001). Between 1940 and 1967, 70% of the top US executives worked for the same company throughout their careers, while in 1990–2003, that fraction declined to 30% (Frydman 2007). Boustanifar et al. (2017) found that high wages in the finance sector do attract skilled workers across borders, and this raises concerns that it may lead to a "brain drain". This effect is not present for unskilled workers, which is likely due to there being greater barriers to their migration relative

---

[2]Bolton et al. (2016) studied models in which activities that are more opaque are related to higher informational rent extraction.

to the pecuniary benefit of doing so. This is consistent with recent theories that stress the role of firm-to-firm mobility in finance workers, which is likely to be easier in such environments. For example, Acharya et al. (2016) studied a model in which an increase in firm-to-firm mobility causes employers to provide excessive short-term compensation, while the employees bear excessive long-term risk. They argue that competition for managerial talent leads to a misallocation of talent by hampering employers' ability to learn the true skills of bankers, traders and managers and, consequently, to allocate them efficiently across projects on risk-taking. Bijlsma et al. (2012), Thanassoulis (2012), and Bénabou and Tirole (2016) studied models in which competition between banks leads to competition for banker talent, which manifests as high banker compensation and incentive pay (bonuses) and unnecessarily high (long-run) risk for banks. In a similar vein, Glode and Lowery (2016) argue that competition for traders—as opposed to bankers, who increase surpluses—is associated with higher rents and reduced social efficiency. They argue that since a trader's expertise improves his employer's ability to appropriate the surplus in a zero-sum trading game, hiring traders imposes something akin to a negative externality on future trading counterparties. This leads to defensive bidding by firms that offer traders a "defensive premium" above their internal marginal product. Without such a premium, traders are firm targets for hire by rival firms, and their expertise could be used against their previous firm. These mechanisms can be triggered, or intensified, by deregulation, with stronger effects in environments that facilitate firm-to-firm mobility.

In addition to the causes and mechanism mentioned above, there are two characteristics (and their combination) specific to financial sector jobs which together raise large moral hazard problems. First, it is hard to monitor the exact effort that an employee puts into many finance jobs. Second, one employee may oversee a large amount of capital, making it important that employees take sufficient care. Moreover, Axelson and Bond (2015) explain the threat of moral hazard associated with high wages and rents in finance by showing that smart workers are "too hard to manage" because their high outside options make them insensitive to the threat of dismissal. In contrast, Célérier and Vallée (2015) argue that talent plays a more important role than moral hazard problems in driving the level of compensation in the sector, in line with talent-based models like that of Thanassoulis (2012).

Additional distinguishing characteristics of financial sector careers are extreme work hours, high reliance on bonuses and "up-or-out" career structures. Generous pay is compensation for the notoriously tough and stressful conditions of many financial sector jobs (e.g., Michel 2011; Bertrand et al. 2010). In addition, pay is highly variable, job security is low and firms rely heavily on up-or-out career structures. For instance, Bell and Van Reenen (2013) show that the growth in bonuses observed over the last decade in the financial industry, particularly for bankers, has gone hand-in-hand with a significant increase in the amount of bonuses as a share of total wages, particularly for those at the top of the wage distribution. In 2008, top percentile workers employed in the UK finance industry received 44% of their total pay as bonuses. With regard to job security, the careers of finance workers tend to be riskier, in line with the fact that financial firms typically carry more risk than nonfinancial ones; hence, the wage profiles of finance workers are 8% more dispersed than those of non-finance ones (Philippon and Reshef 2012). Ellul et al. (2016) show that while some employees rise quickly to the top, others make limited progress, and some even experience permanent setbacks, especially those with recently liquidated hedge funds. Oyer's (2008) estimates of lifetime pay premiums upon entering finance explicitly account for the risk of exiting the sector. Consequently, instead of explaining high pay, the unusual work conditions pose puzzles of their own. With regards to up-or-out careers, financial market shocks have been shown to have important and lasting effects on investment bankers' careers. Oyer (2008) reports that a buoyant stock market encourages MBA students to go directly into investment banking upon graduation, which in turn has a huge and lasting effect on their career choices and earnings. If an individual fails to land a job in the financial sector upon graduation solely because Wall Street is down, he is unlikely to enter the sector later in life when Wall Street has recovered. Given the attractive compensation of financial sector jobs, this pattern of entry is puzzling, since one might expect people to try very hard to enter the finance sector even later in their careers. In other words, these labour markets appear to be dynamically segregated, in that employees can only enter the high-paying sector when young, so that the state of the economy upon graduation has life-long implications.

In this monograph, we will focus on a specific industry subsector—banking. Among the other subsectors, this sector is the most highly regulated, and plays prominent roles in the financial stability of both the financial industry itself and the entire economy. Moreover, since the global financial crisis, the topic of the high pay levels of banking CEOs has attracted public attention.

2.2 Bank CEO Incentives and the Role of Regulation

In the previous section, we discussed the soaring nature of executive compensation in the financial industry, its contribution to rising income inequality across different industries including the financial sector itself, and the causes and mechanisms of this phenomenon. In this section, we focus on the incentives provided to banking CEOs to run firms and their interference with regulatory intervention.

Executive compensation (or executive pay) is a complex topic and is a key mechanism of corporate governance that is carefully designed to attract, retain and motivate CEOs and senior management. Jensen and Murphy (1990) study certainly marked the beginning of a vast body of literature on executive compensation and firm performance. They point out that what matters in executive compensation is not only *how much* we pay top managers but, more importantly, *how* CEOs and top managers are paid. This view emphasises that executive pay contractual structures could have significant economic consequences and affect how shareholders address conflicts of interests and resulting agency costs. Thus, executive compensation contracts, as well as other corporate governance mechanisms (internal and external), are intended to manage agency problems between shareholders as well as other firm's stakeholders.

When information asymmetries about a firm's performance and growth opportunities are relevant, shareholders must handle the two basic problems of adverse selection and moral hazard. In the first, ex-ante the job contract, they are under pressure to recruit and retain good managers. To manage the second, ex-post the job contract, they have to motivate managers to make decisions and take actions that maximise firm value and shareholder wealth. This classic shareholder-management agency problem arises particularly in firms with more dispersed ownership structures.[3] As a matter of fact, a manager, as a utility maximising agent, self-interested and risk-adverse, may find in many instances that is more efficient to pursue his own interests at the expense of shareholder value. This outcome will be more frequently observed when the monitoring of managers is difficult and costly because of information asymmetries and the complexities of firm technology.

In principle, an executive's pay contract should be based on the most informative indicator(s) of whether the executive has taken actions that maximise shareholder value (Holmström 1979, 1982). In reality, because shareholders are unlikely to know which actions are value-maximising, incentive contracts are often directly based on the principals' ultimate objective (i.e., shareholder value). An important mechanism to mitigate the shareholder-management agency problem is through incentive compensation, i.e., by tying managerial compensation to shareholder wealth. Jensen and Meckling (1976) posit that paying CEOs with firm equity, instead of fixed compensation in the form of a salary, motivates managers to exert effort and undertake risk-increasing but positive net present value (NPV) projects that increase shareholder value.

In levered firms, however, aligning managerial incentives with shareholders' interests tends to encourage excessive risk-taking and generates shareholder-debtholder conflicts. This view relies on option pricing theory to explain the different payoffs of a firm's basic financial claims, debt and equity (Black and Scholes 1973; Merton 1973). The value of the stock in a levered firm resembles the value of a long call option contract. As in any option contract, the option value is an increasing function of the underlying asset's volatility. Thus, shareholders will favour more risky investments and will have risk-shifting incentives, i.e., the incentive to take excessive risk at the expense of different claimholders, such as bondholders and creditors. This issue is particularly troublesome for banks because financial institutions have very high leverage ratios (Esty 1997, 1998) and they can alter the risk composition of their assets more quickly than most nonfinancial industries (Levine 2004). Thus, while the shareholders' interest is served and the agency costs of equity decline with efficient equity-based pay contracts, with increasing debt financing we observe a corresponding increase in another type of agency cost, i.e. the agency costs of debt (John and John 1993). In other words, managers who are aligned more with shareholders are more likely to undertake riskier projects that could hurt debtholders. Clearly,

[3]Evidence by Hasan and Song (2012) shows that ownership structures vary across banks. While more than 90% of banks in the US are widely held, in other countries, more than 50% of banks have controlling shareholders with more than 10% shares, which is consistent with the findings based on a large bank sample provided by Caprio et al. (2007).

debtholders are generally concerned about a firm's risk choice and the consequent increase in agency costs of debt.[4] In the banking industry, the conflict arising from this mechanism is further aggravated by two elements: the government deposit insurance system and implicit bailout policies, which act as taxpayer-funded put options (Merton 1977). Bank shareholders may maximise the value of this put by engaging in additional risk-taking at the expense of banks creditors and the deposit insurer. The primary debtholders for a bank are its depositors. Under the government deposit insurance system, a large proportion of deposits are fully insured. Therefore, depositors do not have an incentive to monitor banks vigorously. Instead, the subordinated debtholders of a bank have incentives to monitor the bank's risk choice. As claimants on junior and uninsured debts, subordinated debtholders stand to suffer heavy losses in the case of bank insolvency. Therefore, only subordinated debtholders have the incentive to monitor the bank closely and on an on-going basis. Moreover, regulators will also monitor a bank's risk choice because they have the responsibility to maintain a stable financial system and because the deposit insurance is equivalent to a put option given to the depositors. Thus, subordinated debtholders and bank regulators will provide outside monitoring of the bank's risk choice. However, while they are primarily concerned with the risk of the bank and that of its securities, they may lack the incentives and capabilities to monitor the agency problems between shareholders and managers.

Given these arguments, it becomes crucial that the board of directors—another important internal corporate governance mechanism—performs its role to design incentives that align CEOs' best interests with those of both shareholders and debtholders while considering the effect of alternative regulatory and monitoring mechanisms.

Incentives are determined by different components of CEOs' compensation structures (Aggarwal 2008; Hagendorff and Srivastav 2016). There are incentives that come from short-term components of compensation, such as cash bonuses, and others that come from long-term components of compensation. These can be categorised as equity-and debt-based compensation. Equity-based compensation includes restricted stock option grants and stock grants, which are usually vested for several years, while debt-based compensation consists of deferred compensation and pension benefits.

With regard to cash bonuses, as long as they increase linearly with corporate performance, the payoffs linked to a bonus plan are non-convex and, therefore, not inherently risk-rewarding (Smith and Stulz (1985)). However, when performance is below the earnings-based threshold at which bonuses become payable, bonus plans resemble a call option on the performance measure. In this case, bonus plan payoffs will be convex and offset the concavity of the CEO's risk-averse utility function. Moreover, since CEO cash bonuses are only paid in states of solvency, CEOs at

[4] Certain economic mechanisms may limit the extent of agency costs in debt markets. Beside charging a higher borrowing rate to compensate for any future loss (which it increases firm's cost of capital), bond and loan contracts typically rely on positive and negative covenants to directly or indirectly control managerial actions (Smith and Warner 1979). Furthermore, reputation—both from repeated interactions with debt markets (Diamond 1989) and career concerns of managers (Fama 1980)—discourages managers by engaging in asset substitution and risk-shifting games.

distressed firms may engage in risk-shifting to "gamble for solvency" with little regard for the liquidation value of the firm. When senior management knows that there is a high likelihood a bank could fail, they are likely to undertake riskier strategies in an effort to boost short-term performance. While such behaviour may increase the probability of bank default, managers expect to benefit in terms of continuous employment and future pay should their gamble pay off (Edmans and Liu 2011).

With regard to equity-based compensation, the use of a performance-sensitive compensation structure is consistent with the agency theory of aligning the interests of risk-adverse managers with those of risk-neutral shareholders. Equity instruments result in the embedding of two types of incentives. First, equity instruments induce CEOs to exert greater effort by making their compensation more sensitive to performance (also known as pay-performance sensitivity, PPS, or delta incentives). Second, equity instruments motivate CEOs to pursue risky projects by making their compensation more sensitive to risk (also known as pay-risk sensitivity or vega incentives). Typically, including a large amount of stock grants (and to a lesser extent, stock option grants) in CEO compensation packages will result in high deltas. In fact, bank executives holding common shares in a bank holding company will have an incentive to be more conservative than what is in the interest of other common shareholders. To begin with, to the extent that the ownership of common shares in the bank holding company represents a substantial fraction of an executive's wealth, such a large stake might lead the executive to be more risk-averse than the shareholders, who could be more diversified. In addition, a bank might impose significant personal costs on the bank's managers that would not be borne by other common shareholders. However, there is a problem where short-horizon distortions arise from the freedom to cash equity-based compensation before long-term results are realised.

In contrast, including a large amount of stock option grants in CEO compensation packages will result in high vegas. CEO vega incentives are also associated with higher bank instability and a higher likelihood of engaging in risk-taking investments, indicating that adopting risk-taking incentives in equity contracts could result in the promotion of riskier strategies. With option-based compensation contracts, executives have even more incentive for risk-taking than the common shareholders of bank holding companies. This is explained by the asymmetric payoffs typical of option securities; options limit downside risks while offering the full potential of upside payoffs. Thus, option-based compensation can further exacerbate the moral hazard problem and the incentive to take excessive risks. In fact, a stock option gives the holder the right to acquire a share at some future date for a prespecified price—the "strike price." This right will be valuable if the future stock price is above the strike price but will be worthless otherwise. Consequently, the holder of an option only cares about share price fluctuations above the strike price. It makes no difference to the option holder if the share price ends up being equal to the strike price or far below it.

Compensation incentives are also structured through the use of debt-based compensation, such that managers' incentives are aligned with the interests of creditors, taxpayers and depositors. These instruments resemble debt in two aspects: first, inside debt is a fixed obligation for a firm to make payments to a manager that commence upon retirement and continue throughout it. Second, inside debt is an unsecured firm obligation. In the event of bankruptcy, a manager stands in line with other unsecured creditors to recover some fraction of his inside debt holdings. When the payoffs of CEO wealth are tied to creditors, managers may shift their focus to the long-term solvency of the firm and prevent equity-aligned managers from pursuing policies which increase shareholder wealth at the expense of increasing risk beyond that which is desirable to creditors (Edmans and Liu 2011). When managers own more firm debt than firm equity, it is more likely that they will select prudent policies and reduce the firm's underlying risks.

Overall, when pay arrangements reward top managers for short-term gains and create excessive risk-taking behaviour, executives may have an incentive to focus on short-term gains, even when doing so may adversely affect the expected long-term value of shareholders. Thus, it is not surprising that concerns about incentives for risk-taking in banks have led legislators and regulators to adopt measures aimed at improving internal governance arrangements and preventing managers from working against the goal of prudential regulation. While traditional regulations monitor bank executives through capital adequacy requirements, pay regulation focuses on the incentives that shape how bank executives make their choices. Jointly, the two approaches may reinforce each other and work together to protect the safety and soundness of banks.

In the aftermath of the 2008–2009 financial crisis, regulators in the US and Europe considered and implemented rules designed to curb perceived excesses in the level of banking bonuses and risk-taking incentives in general. However, they followed different approaches. European regulators mostly followed a prescriptive approach that introduced caps on the level and structure of executive pay. In contrast, US regulators followed a more principle-based approach and gave banks greater flexibility in deciding the optimal mix of executive pay.

More specifically, on 16 April 2013, the European Parliament approved the Capital Requirements Directives (CRD-IV), which include bank executive pay restrictions. These new rules became effective as of January 2014. The CRD-IV mandates that variable pay components (including bonuses) are to be capped at 100% of a CEO's fixed remuneration (the ratio of variable-to-fixed remuneration would be capped at 1:1) with the possibility that this threshold can reach 200% (the ratio of variable-to-fixed remuneration could be increased to 2:1) with the backing of a supermajority of shareholders. US regulators followed a principle-based approach by issuing general guidelines to guide banks in deciding their remuneration policies. Among these, the Federal Reserve (2010) issued guidance that outlined key compensation principles for remunerating top executives. The first principle focused on encouraging banks to adopt pay instruments that account for the impact of each executive on overall bank risk, and that take into account the time horizon over which financial risks may materialise. The second and third principles highlighted the role of the risk management division in providing inputs during the pay-setting process, and the role of the board of directors in designing pay structures that ensure an appropriate balance between bank risk and performance. More importantly, banks were urged to tailor compensation policies to the ability of individuals to expose their institutions to extreme negative risk events, and bank complexity and size. Another key development in the US regulatory landscape was the passing of the *Dodd-Frank Wall Street Reform and Consumer Protection Act* (Dodd-Frank Act) in July 2010. Dodd-Frank reiterated the already established principle that banks should limit those types of incentive pay that may result in excessive risk-taking. Moreover, banks were encouraged to disclose the structure of executive compensation to their respective regulatory agencies. Further, Dodd-Frank required shareholder approval through say-on-pay votes and safeguarded the independence of compensation committees. While such policies help in directing remuneration practices in the right direction, they do not directly interfere with or restrict executive pay arrangements. Each bank can decide on compensation based on the idiosyncratic factors that affect them.[5]

2.3 Determinants of Bank CEO Compensation

In the previous section, we discussed the structure of bank CEO compensation, the relative incentives for excessive risk-taking, and some regulatory actions intended to correct CEO behaviour in making decisions that are inconsistent with the goals of prudential regulation. In this section, we describe four interconnected factors which might alter bank executives' incentives: (1) the CEO labour market; (2) CEO pay contracting; (3) CEO characteristics; and (4) banking regulations.

The first determinant is related to the bank CEO labour market. Following the principal-agent theory, pay and risk are correlated, not because misaligned pay leads to risk-taking but, rather, because riskier firms have to increase pay more than less risky firms do to provide risk-averse managers with the same level of incentive. To induce a manager to exert effort and maximise firm value, the principal must provide the manager with attractive incentives or an ownership stake in the firm. For the same level of incentive or ownership stake, a manager with a riskier firm faces much more wealth uncertainty because their firm's performance (e.g. net income and/or market value) is more volatile. As most managers are risk-averse, they will prefer to work for less risky firms, all else equal, unless they are compensated for bearing the additional risk of working for a more risky firm. As such, to provide adequate incentives, a more risky firm has to pay more than a less risky firm. Of course, if it is more expensive for riskier firms to determine managerial incentives using insider ownership stakes then, all else being equal, such firms may find it optimal to offer a smaller insider ownership stake than less risky firms. In practice, however, there are several reasons why even very risky financial firms may want their managers to have ownership stakes as large as those of managers of less risky firms. One important reason is that these firms rely on people with specialised skills (such as managing complex investments) and who wield significant influence over outcomes. When an agent has significant influence over outcomes, it is optimal to keep them working.

[5]For a detailed history of banking compensation regulation see, for instance, Cadman et al. (2012) and Murphy (2013).

The second problem is concerned with determining how to operationalise CEO incentives and compensation to monitor and manage risky behaviour. Jensen and Meckling (1976) argue that compensation should be structured so that the composition of the CEO's holdings of inside debt and inside equity parallels that of the firm's debt and equity holdings. They hypothesise that there is an optimal ratio of the CEO's inside debt-to-equity ratio deflated by the firm's debt-to-equity ratio. In contrast, bank CEOs' pay before the global financial crisis was substantial and mostly performance-based, with an incentive pay structure that resembled the standard wealth-maximising approach to compensation used in unregulated industries. Bennett et al. (2015) reported an average level of inside equity equal to $41 million versus an average level of inside debt equal to $3 million in a sample of 371 CEOs of US bank holding companies. Consistent with the agency view of debt financing, a greater managerial focus on improving shareholder returns could distort investment policy. This will encourage riskier strategies that are against the public interests of bank safety and financial system stability. However, when bank managers' interests are aligned with those of bank equity holders, the moral hazard problem that characterises deposit insurance will be amplified. This result is found in Fahlenbrach and Stulz (2011), who show that better alignment of CEO incentives with shareholder interests was associated with worse bank performance during the 2008 credit crisis. The unintended consequence of badly designed equity incentives leads to an argument that if CEOs were focused mostly on shareholder value maximisation, their risk-taking activities would not be efficient for other bank stakeholders (i.e., the deposit insurer and bondholders). Recently, several proposals have been put forward to shift compensation away from equity-based incentives but, rather, to also link them to the federal deposit insurance premium (John et al. 2000), the value of debt-like instruments (Bebchuk and Spamann 2010), a bank's credit default swap spread (Bolton et al. 2015), the pricing of government guarantees (Carpenter et al. 2011) or to give more power to debtholders rather than shareholders (van Bekkum 2016). With regard to the bonus-risk relationship, Vallascas and Hagendorff (2013) show that increases in CEO cash bonuses lower banks' default risk. This occurs because bonus payments can only be received in a state of solvency, forcing CEOs to avoid financial distress or even outright bankruptcy (Brander and Poitevin 1992). Moreover, especially in the presence of asymmetric information on manager quality, bonuses could also be considered as a tool to attract talented candidates (Bannier et al. 2013). Attracting good managers with high bonus schemes is cheaper than with flat contracts. This finding challenges the view underlying the regulatory actions regarding cash-based executive compensation. A regulatory cap on bonuses for banks can then have negative effects. High-type managers can be cheaply poached by non-banks, maybe even by financial institutions from the unregulated shadow banking sector. Competition for managers may push "high-type" bank managers to other economic sectors, which may (or may not) be desirable from a welfare perspective.

The third determinant of CEO incentives is their personal characteristics, the way they vary among different types of banks, and whether they are relevant in bank management. The idea that individual heterogeneity matters in corporate finance has recently attracted the attention of behavioural finance scholars.[6] Recent papers suggest that managers' characteristics matter. Empirical findings suggest there are significant managerial fixed effects (Bertrand and Schoar 2003), originating from overconfidence (Malmendier and Tate 2005, 2008), narcissism (Ham et al. 2017), past military service (Benmelech and Frydman 2015), records of legal infractions (Davidson et al. 2015), whether their career started during economic growth or recession (Schoar and Zuo 2017), religious belief (Hilary and Hui 2009), political preferences (Hutton et al. 2014), optimism and risk-aversion (Graham et al. 2013), sensation seeking (Cain and McKeon 2016), the hobby of flying airplanes (Sunder et al. 2017), and cultural heritage (Nguyen et al. 2018). The observed outcome, even within a rather homogeneous financial industry, is that similar banks, with matched characteristics, could perform differently. Moreover, it is also well known that observationally equivalent individuals often earn markedly different levels of compensation. Different levels of compensation could occur because of unobservable firm characteristics, such as corporate culture, or partially because of unobserved personal characteristics such as innate ability or personality. Hence, the literature has started to question how much managers' characteristics explain the observed variability in their compensation (Graham et al. 2012). The intuition is that CEO-specific attributes may act as a channel through which CEOs can influence risk management strategies and corporate culture. More specifically, educational level, overconfidence, a materialist attitude, and CEO power have been investigated in relation to attitudes towards risky behaviour. King et al. (2016) show that banks led by CEOs with better MBA scores achieve greater profitability than banks headed by non-MBA CEOs. Moreover, CEOs with better MBA education who follow riskier and more innovative business models secure superior bank performance outcomes. Such CEOs, when offered larger incentives to increase stock price volatility, or if their compensation structure contains greater equity incentives, appear able to mitigate potentially adverse outcomes associated with excessive risk-taking and deliver significantly higher bank profitability. In contrast, by underestimating the downside risk of a project, an overconfident CEO tends to choose riskier investments. Evidence indicates that banks managed by overconfident CEOs have higher standard deviations in stock returns (Niu 2010), experience greater default risk (Burg et al. 2012), and grant more real estate loans (Ma 2014). Ho et al. (2016) extended previous studies to show that overconfidence can lead risk-averse CEOs to take exposures that they perceive are most profitable for current shareholders ex-ante, but could harm their banks and themselves ex-post. Banks managed by overconfident CEOs tend to approve more loans and assume more leverage than non-overconfident banks before financial crises. However, during crisis years, they experienced worse operating and stock return performance, greater increases in expected default probability, and a higher likelihood of CEO turnover or failure. Ho et al. (2016) also show that overconfident CEOs, who typically pursue riskier strategies during times of economic growth, are more likely to be hired by banks with an aggressive risk culture. Humphery-Jenner et al. (2016) went further to show that

[6]See Baker and Wurgler (2013) for a survey of behavioral corporate finance issues and their implications for investment and financing patterns.

overconfidence also affects the compensation structure of CEOs: overconfident CEOs receive more option-intensive compensation contracts. Moreover, option intensity is greater for overconfident CEOs at riskier firms and more innovative firms. Bushman et al. (2017) documented an upward trend in the number of US banks run by materialistic CEOs around a time of major bank deregulation (1994–2004). This result was not found for non-financial firms and other CEO characteristics examined in the literature. Banks run by materialistic CEOs have significantly more downside tail risk and tail risk co-movement with aggregate tail risk shocks relative to non-materialistic CEOs. Further, while they found that materialistic CEOs are associated with higher downside tail risk, they are also associated with higher tail rewards. It follows that financial deregulation provoked a sector-wide shift in the prominence of materialistic CEOs that became a major problem for prudential regulation. Mollah and Liljeblom (2016) found that CEO power had a positive relationship with bank profitability and asset quality, but also to insolvency risk, during the sovereign debt crisis. Moreover, Onali et al. (2016) show that entrenched CEOs do not have a strong incentive to pay dividends because of a combination of weak minority shareholder regulation, an inefficient market for corporate control and government concerns about bank soundness.

The fourth determinant of bank CEO compensation is financial regulation. Poor executive incentives have frequently been identified as a cause of the global financial crisis. As a result, new legislation has expanded the rights of shareholders in approving compensation practices, appointing directors on compensation committees, and designing compensation proposals. For instance, the Corporate and Financial Institution Compensation Fairness Act of 2009 expanded the rights of shareholders in approving compensation practices and appointing directors to compensation committees. In 2010, the *Dodd-Frank Wall Street Reform and Consumer Protection Act* of 2010 mandated shareholders to vote on executive compensation and empowered them to design their own compensation proposals. Similar international initiatives also adopt a shareholder-friendly governance perspective, such as the *Principles and Implementations Standards for Sound Compensation Practices* of the Financial Stability Forum, which represents G-20 finance ministries and central bankers. However, notwithstanding increased scrutiny from regulators and legislators, the academic evidence on whether shareholder governance actually limits bank risk is still not convincing. Moreover, regulation mandating explicit restrictions on the level of managerial compensation has unintended consequences (Perry and Zenner 2001; Murphy 2011)) and is not supported by the empirical evidence to-date, which is inconclusive about whether average CEO pay is too high or too low (Faulkender et al. 2010). Regarding bonus components, the regulatory regime might have an impact on the bonus-risk relationship as the risk-reducing incentives embedded in CEO bonus plans might be counterweighted by incentives for banks to shift risk to regulators, which are weak. Hakenes and Schnabel (2014) show that bonus restrictions are desirable in financial systems with weak regulatory frameworks and no credible resolution procedures. Many observers consider it unfair that banks paid out high bonuses after suffering unprecedented losses and being bailed out by the government. This led to the question of whether regulatory constraints are good for all banks or only some of them. It has been found that attitudes toward risk-taking vary systematically among banks. Risk is considered more acceptable for systemically important financial institutions (SIFIs) for which (implicit) bailout guarantees—and thus risk-shifting incentives—are stronger; and for banks that gain a large percentage of their income from non-traditional banking activities that are highly affected by technological innovation and for which raising risk is less costly than for traditional banks. Moreover, such an attitude is stronger when a bank is in distress, as CEOs seek to maximise the value of the financial safety net. Vallascas and Hagendorff (2013) and Hakenes and Schnabel (2014) support the view that regulatory interference, such as ceilings on bonus payments, is the preferred method of preventing excessive risk-taking, especially for these banks. Since bonuses are linked to higher bank risk-taking at the riskiest banks, risk-shifting incentives at these institutions are only likely to be constrained if compensation practices more closely align the interests of managers and debt-holders. In contrast, measures that increase managers' liability, such as deferrals of bonuses and clawback clauses, are still questionable. Attitudes toward risk-taking vary systematically across banks, implying that "one size of government intervention may not fit all". Such results suggest that government intervention that restricts executive compensation will have the most social value if it targets the very largest banks, which have strong growth opportunities and histories of providing highly aggressive risk-taking incentives to their CEOs. Hubbard and Palia (1995) and DeYoung et al. (2013) found that government intervention to limit risk-taking incentives in financial executive compensation contracts could at best strengthen, and at worst interfere with, the role of boards in monitoring risk levels at firms. Having evaluated firm risk, a board may attempt to influence it by changing the CEO's incentives (e.g., vega and delta). However, such internal monitoring is absent at the very largest banks and, again, regulatory intervention is desirable.

References

Acharya, V., M. Pagano, and P. Volpin. 2016. Seeking alpha: Excess risk taking and competition for managerial talent. *Review of Financial Studies* 29 (10): 2565–2599.

Aggarwal, R.K. 2008. Executive compensation and incentives. In *Handbook of Corporate Finance: Empirical Corporate Finance*, ed. B.E. Eckbo, 497–538. North Holland: Elsevier.

Axelson, U.L.F., and P. Bond. 2015. Wall street occupations. *Journal of Finance* 70 (5): 1949–1996.

Baker, M., and J. Wurgler. 2013. Behavioral corporate finance: An updated survey. In *Handbook of the Economics of Finance*, ed. G.M. Constantinides, M. Harris, and S. Rene, 357–424. Amsterdam: North Holland.

Bannier, C.E., E. Feess, and N. Packham. 2013. Competition, bonuses, and risk-taking in the banking industry. *Review of Finance* 17 (2): 653–690.

Bebchuk, L.A., and H. Spamann. 2010. Regulating banker's pay. *Georgetown Law Journal* 98: 247–287.

Bell, B., and J. Van Reenen. 2013. Bankers and their bonuses. *Economic Journal* 124 (574): F1–F21.

Bénabou, R., and J. Tirole. 2016. Bonus culture: Competitive pay, screening, and multitasking. *Journal of Political Economy* 124 (2): 305–370.

Bennett, R.L., L. Güntay, and H. Unal. 2015. Inside debt, bank default risk, and performance during the crisis. *Journal of Financial Intermediation* 24 (4): 487–513.

Benmelech, E., and C. Frydman. 2015. Military CEOs. *Journal of Financial Economics* 117 (1): 43–59.
Berger, A.N., N.H. Miller, M.A. Petersen, R.G. Rajan, and J.C. Stein. 2005. Does function follow organizational form? Evidence from the lending practices of large and small banks. *Journal of Financial Economics* 76 (2): 237–269.
Bertrand, M., C. Goldin, and L.F. Katz. 2010. Dynamics of the gender gap for young professionals in the financial and corporate sectors. *American Economic Journal: Applied Economics* 2 (3): 228–255.
Bertrand, M., and A. Schoar. 2003. Managing with Style: The Effect of Managers on Firm Policies. *The Quarterly Journal of Economics* 118 (4): 1169–1208.
Bijlsma, M.J., J. Boone, and G. Zwart. 2012. Competition for traders and risk. CentER discussion paper, Tilburg University.
Bivens, J., and L. Mishel. 2013. The pay of corporate executives and financial professionals as evidence of rents in top 1 percent incomes. *Journal of Economic Perspectives* 27 (3): 57–77.
Black, F., and M. Scholes. 1973. The pricing of options and corporate liabilities. *Journal of Political Economy* 81 (3): 637–654.
Bolton, P., H. Mehran, and J. Shapiro. 2015. Executive compensation and risk taking. *Review of Finance* 19 (6): 2139–2181.
Bolton, P., T. Santos, and J.A. Scheinkman. 2016. Cream-skimming in financial markets. *Journal of Finance* 71 (2): 709–736.
Boustanifar, H., E. Grant, and A. Reshef. 2017. Wages and human capital in finance: International evidence, 1970–2011. *Review of Finance* rfx011.
Brander, J.A., and M. Poitevin. 1992. Managerial compensation and the agency costs of debt finance. *Managerial and Decision Economics* 13 (1): 55–64.
Burg, V., T. Scheinert, and D. Streitz. 2012. Bank CEO overconfidence and risk-taking. Working paper, Humboldt University of Berlin.
Bushman, R.M., R.H. Davidson, A. Dey, and A.J. Smith. 2017. Bank CEO materialism: Risk controls, culture and tail risk. Georgetown McDonough School of Business Research Paper.
Cadman, B., M.E. Carter, and L.J. Lynch. 2012. Executive compensation restrictions: Do they restrict firms' willingness to participate in TARP? *Journal of Business Finance & Accounting* 39 (7–8): 997–1027.
Cain, M.D., and S.B. McKeon. 2016. CEO personal risk-taking and corporate policies. *Journal of Financial and Quantitative Analysis* 51 (1): 139–164.
Caprio, G., L. Laeven, and R. Levine. 2007. Governance and bank valuation. *Journal of Financial Intermediation* 16 (4): 584–617.
Carpenter, J., T. Cooley, and I. Walter. 2011. Reforming compensation and corporate governance. In *Regulating Wall Street: The Dodd-Frank Act and the New Architecture of Global Finance*, ed. V.V. Acharya, T.F. Cooley, M. Richardson and I. Walter, 491–509. Hoboken, NJ, USA: Wiley.
Célérier, C., and B. Vallée. 2015. Returns to talent and the finance wage premium. Working paper, Harvard Business School.
Davidson, R., A. Dey, and A. Smith. 2015. 'Executives' "off-the-job" behavior, corporate culture, and financial reporting risk. *Journal of Financial Economics* 117 (1): 5–28.
DeYoung, R., E.Y. Peng, and M. Yan. 2013. Executive compensation and business policy choices at U.S. Commercial Banks. *Journal of Financial and Quantitative Analysis* 48 (1): 165–196.
Diamond, D.W. 1989. Reputation acquisition in debt markets. *Journal of Political Economy* 97 (4): 828–862.
Edmans, A., and Q. Liu. 2011. Inside debt. *Review of Finance* 15 (1): 75–102.
Ellul, A., M. Pagano, and A. Scognamiglio. 2016. Careers in finance. Working paper, Center for Studies in Economics and Finance.
Esty, B.C. 1997. Organizational form and risk taking in the savings and loan industry. *Journal of Financial Economics* 44 (1): 25–55.
Esty, B.C. 1998. The impact of contingent liability on commercial bank risk taking. *Journal of Financial Economics* 47 (2): 189–218.

Fahlenbrach, R., and R.M. Stulz. 2011. Bank CEO incentives and the credit crisis. *Journal of Financial Economics* 99 (1): 11–26.

Fama, E.F. 1980. Agency problems and the theory of the firm. *Journal of Political Economy* 88 (2): 288–307.

Faulkender, M., D. Kadyrzhanova, N. Prabhala, and L. Senbet. 2010. Executive compensation: An overview of research on corporate practices and proposed reforms. *Journal of Applied Corporate Finance* 22 (1): 107–118.

Frydman, C. 2007. Rising through the ranks. The evolution of the market for corporate executives 1936–2003. MIT Working Paper.

Glode, V., and R. Lowery. 2016. Compensating financial experts. *Journal of Finance* 71 (6): 2781–2808.

Goodhart, C., P. Hartmann, D.T. Llewellyn, L. Rojas-Suarez, and S. Weisbrod. 1998. *Financial Regulation: Why, How and Where Now?*. London: Routledge.

Graham, J.R., S. Li, and J. Qiu. 2012. Managerial attributes and executive compensation. *Review of Financial Studies* 25 (1): 144–186.

Graham, J.R., Campbell, R.H., and M. Puri. 2013. Managerial attitudes and corporate actions. *Journal of Financial Economics* 109 (1): 103–121.

Hagendorff, J., and A. Srivastav. 2016. Pay structures in European Banks. In *Handbook of European Banking*, ed. T. Beck, and B. Casu, 135–155. Palgrave MacMillan: Basingstoke.

Hakenes, H., and I. Schnabel. 2014. Bank bonuses and bailouts. *Journal of Money, Credit and Banking* 46 (s1): 259–288.

Ham, C., M. Lang, N. Seybert, and S. Wang. 2017. CFO narcissism and financial reporting quality. *Journal of Accounting Research*.

Hasan, I., and L. Song. 2012. Bank ownership and performance: A global perspective. In *Research Handbook on International Banking and Governance*, ed. J. Barth, C. Lin, and C. Wihlborg, 42–71. Cheltenham: Edward Elgar Publishing Ltd.

Hilary, G., and K.W. Hui. 2009. Does religion matter in corporate decision making in America? *Journal of Financial Economics* 93 (3): 455–473.

Ho, P.-H., C.-W. Huang, C.-Y. Lin, and J.-F. Yen. 2016. CEO overconfidence and financial crisis: Evidence from bank lending and leverage. *Journal of Financial Economics* 120 (1): 194–209.

Holmström, B. 1979. Moral hazard and observability. *Bell Journal of Economics* 74–91.

Holmström. 1982. Moral hazard in teams. *Bell Journal of Economics* 324–340.

Hubbard, R.G., and D. Palia. 1995. Executive pay and performance Evidence from the U.S. banking industry. *Journal of Financial Economics* 39 (1): 105–130.

Humphery-Jenner, M., L.L. Lisic, V. Nanda, and S.D. Silveri. 2016. Executive overconfidence and compensation structure. *Journal of Financial Economics* 119 (3): 533–558.

Huson, M.R., R. Parrino, and L.T. Starks. 2001. Internal monitoring mechanisms and CEO turnover: A long-term perspective. *Journal of Finance* 56 (6): 2265–2297.

Hutton, I., D. Jiang, and A. Kumar. 2014. Corporate policies of republican managers. *Journal of Financial and Quantitative Analysis* 49 (5–6): 1279–1310.

Ibert, M., R. Kaniel, S. Van Nieuwerburgh, and R. Vestman. 2017. Are mutual fund managers paid for investment skill? Working paper, National Bureau of Economic Research.

Jensen, M.C., and W.H. Meckling. 1976. Theory of the firm: Managerial behavior, agency costs and ownership structure. *Journal of Financial Economics* 3 (4): 305–360.

Jensen, M.C., and K.J. Murphy. 1990. Performance pay and top-management incentives. *Journal of Political Economy* 98 (2): 225–264.

John, K., A. Saunders, and L.W. Senbet. 2000. A theory of bank regulation and management compensation. *Review of Financial Studies* 13 (1): 95–125.

John, T.A., and K. John. 1993. Top-management compensation and capital structure. *Journal of Finance* 48 (3): 949–974.

Kaplan, S.N., and J. Rauh. 2009. Wall street and main street: What contributes to the rise in the highest incomes? *Review of Financial Studies* 23 (3): 1004–1050.

King, T., A. Srivastav, and J. Williams. 2016. What's in an education? Implications of CEO education for bank performance. *Journal of Corporate Finance* 37: 287–308.

Korinek, A., and J. Kreamer. 2014. The redistributive effects of financial deregulation. *Journal of monetary Economics* 68: S55–S67.

Levine, R. 2004. *The corporate governance of banks: A concise discussion of concepts and evidence*, vol. 3404. World Bank Publications.

Lindley, J., and S. McIntosh. 2017. Finance sector wage growth and the role of human capital. *Oxford Bulletin of Economics and Statistics* 79 (4): 570–591.

Ma, Y. 2014. Bank CEO optimism and the financial crisis. Working paper, Harvard University.

Malmendier, U., and G. Tate. 2005. CEO overconfidence and corporate investment. *Journal of Finance* 60 (6): 2661–2700.

Malmendier, U., and G. Tate. 2008. Who makes acquisitions? CEO overconfidence and the market's reaction. *Journal of Financial Economics* 89 (1): 20–43.

Merton, R.C. 1973. Theory of rational option pricing. *Bell Journal of Economics and Management Science* 141–183.

Merton, R.C. 1977. An analytic derivation of the cost of deposit insurance and loan guarantees an application of modern option pricing theory. *Journal of Banking & Finance* 1 (1):3–11.

Michel, A. 2011. Transcending socialization: A nine-year ethnography of the body's role in organizational control and knowledge workers' transformation. *Administrative Science Quarterly* 56 (3): 325–368.

Mollah, S., and E. Liljeblom. 2016. Governance and bank characteristics in the credit and sovereign debt crises—The impact of CEO power. *Journal of Financial Stability* 27: 59–73.

Morrison, A.D., and W.J. Wilhelm. 2008. The demise of investment banking partnerships: Theory and evidence. *Journal of Finance* 63 (1): 311–350.

Murphy, K.J. 2011. The politics of pay: A legislative history of executive compensation. In *Research Handbook on Executive Pay*, ed. J. Hill, and R. Thomas. Cheltenham: Edward Elagar.

Murphy, K.J. 2013. Regulating banking bonuses in the European Union: A case study in unintended consequences. *European Financial Management* 19 (4): 631–657.

Nguyen, D.D., J. Hagendorff, and A. Eshraghi. 2018. Does a CEO's cultural heritage affect performance under competitive pressure? *The Review of Financial Studies* 31 (1): 97–141.

Niu, J. 2010. The effect of CEO overconfidence on bank risk taking. *Economics Bulletin* 30 (4): 3288–3299.

Onali, E., R. Galiakhmetova, P. Molyneux, and G. Torluccio. 2016. CEO power, government monitoring, and bank dividends. *Journal of Financial Intermediation* 27: 89–117.

Oyer, P. 2008. The making of an investment banker: Stock market shocks, career choice, and lifetime income. *Journal of Finance* 63 (6): 2601–2628.

Perry, T., and M. Zenner. 2001. Pay for performance? Government regulation and the structure of compensation contracts. *Journal of Financial Economics* 62 (3): 453–488.

Petersen, M.A., and R.G. Rajan. 2002. Does distance still matter? The information revolution in small business lending. *Journal of Finance* 57 (6): 2533–2570.

Philippon, T., and A. Reshef. 2012. Wages and human capital in the US finance industry: 1909–2006. *Quarterly Journal of Economics* 127 (4): 1551–1609.

Schoar, A., and L. Zuo. 2017. Shaped by booms and busts: How the economy impacts CEO careers and management styles. *Review of Financial Studies* 30 (5): 1425–1456.

Smith, C., and J. Warner. 1979. On financial contracting: An analysis of bond covenants. *Journal of Financial Economics* 7 (2): 117–161.

Smith, C.W., and R.M. Stulz. 1985. The determinants of firms' hedging policies. *Journal of Financial and Quantitative Analysis* 20 (4): 391–405.

Sunder, J., S.V. Sunder, and J. Zhang. 2017. Pilot CEOs and corporate innovation. *Journal of Financial Economics* 123 (1): 209–224.
Thanassoulis, J. 2012. The case for intervening in bankers' pay. *Journal of Finance* 67 (3): 849–895.
Vallascas, F., and J. Hagendorff. 2013. CEO bonus compensation and bank default risk: Evidence from the US and Europe. *Financial Markets, Institutions & Instruments* 22 (2): 47–89.
van Bekkum, S. 2016. Inside debt and bank risk. *Journal of Financial and Quantitative Analysis* 51 (2): 359–385.

Chapter 3
Theory and Stylised Facts of Bank CEO Pay Consequences

Abstract If bank CEOs are special, as each bank is, do the characteristics of banks influence the ways that CEOs make complex and non-routine strategic decisions? Do CEOs leave their mark or have a personal style when making investment, financing and other strategic decisions? Moreover, given the incentives for risk-taking implicit in CEO remuneration contracts, how do these incentives interact with unobservable CEO characteristics? In this Chapter, we review the major theoretical and empirical findings of the literature, highlighting how different CEO characteristics (personal and acquired) contribute to performance and risk-taking. We present empirical evidence of the sensitivity of CEO pay to bank performance and risk in pre-crisis years, and the role it played in causing the recent financial crisis. We discuss contrasting findings, highlighting the debated relationship between pre-crisis CEO incentives to take risks and crisis-period bank performance. We then discuss the main regulatory interventions undertaken in response to this issue, and their suitability in light of recent banking CEO compensation models. We conclude this chapter with a description of CEO incentives in relation to strategic decisions, such as mergers and acquisitions and restructuring programs, and how these may influence bank performance and risk.

3.1 CEO Characteristics and Performance Consequences

The previous chapter's discussion clearly indicates that banks are complex institutions that require employees with specialised skills. Banking decisions are likely to be complex, non-routine and unstructured, and CEO characteristics are, therefore, likely to be salient in how CEOs make decisions. Moreover, selecting the right executives is crucial for banks, as CEOs (and employees as well) have their own "styles" when making investment, financing and other strategic decisions, thereby imprinting their personal marks on the companies they manage (Bertrand and Schoar 2003; Malmendier and Tate 2005, 2008; Fee et al. 2013; Graham et al. 2013). Overall, since CEOs are responsible for the day-to-day running of banks and have discretion over their decisions, it is likely that their "style" affects the performance of banks,

C. Curi and M. Murgia, *Bank CEOs*, SpringerBriefs in Finance,
https://doi.org/10.1007/978-3-319-90866-3_3

in addition to the effects of firm, industry or market characteristics.[1] In this section, we discuss two groups of bank CEO characteristics. The first group includes the personal (innate) characteristics of CEOs such as their age, job experience, education, confidence and cultural heritage. The second group describes the characteristics of the corporate governance mechanisms of banks that CEOs acquire through their employment, which include CEO power and CEO turnover.

The empirical question of whether or not individual executives' characteristics affect corporate outcomes challenges neoclassical and agency theories. The first assumes that individuals are homogenous, such that different executives can be perfect substitutes for each other. The second sees executives' actions as shaped by the quality of corporate governance in the organisation. It is closely related to management theory and Hambrick and Mason (1984) upper echelons. Nguyen et al. (2015) demonstrated that executives' ancestral origins influenced bank market returns (i.e. creating wealth for shareholders) in a sample of executives newly appointed by US banks between 1999 and 2011. The CEO characteristics that contribute most to value creation are related to older age, prior experience as an executive director, and the holding of an Ivy League degree. By contrast, appointments of executives holding multiple non-executive directorships result in negative returns. In addition, the gender of the appointee and their experience in non-banking industries do not affect stock market returns around the appointment announcement of a new executive. However, in line with agency theory, the positive wealth effect linked to an appointment diminishes with increased board monitoring and non-executive director involvement in board decision-making.

Another important effect of unobservable personal CEO characteristics is their interaction with the risk-taking incentives that are implicit in the structure of executive compensation contracts, which ultimately determine bank performance outcomes. Crucially, the responsiveness of executives to their equity incentives, and their choices of risky policies, may be determined by their educational background (Bertrand and Schoar 2003; Beber and Fabbri 2012). In particular, management education could enable CEOs to manage the risk-taking incentives that are inherent in compensation contracts, because it confers the general managerial skills that enable CEOs to deliver superior performance outcomes at larger and more complex businesses (see Frydman 2007). Using a sample of CEOs of publicly-listed US banks during 1992–2011, King et al. (2016) found results consistent with the emerging consensus in the literature—that the education of CEOs is a factor in explaining performance differentials. More specifically, bank CEOs with higher MBA education factors (i.e. level and quality of management education) typically exhibit better firm performance, but undergraduate and Ph.D. qualifications do not appear to matter.[2] Moreover, CEOs with higher MBA education factors are more likely to improve bank

[1]There is much empirical literature on CEO characteristics and the performance of nonfinancial firms (e.g., Adams et al. 2005; Custódio and Metzger 2013; Custódio et al. 2013; Kaplan et al. 2012).

[2]This effect is also economically meaningful, with a one standard deviation in MBA education resulting in improved performance by 11.4% relative to the mean.

performance in response to higher risk-taking incentives (notably, vega incentives to increase the volatility of stock price returns), such as receiving a higher fraction of equity compensation in their compensation structure. In other words, CEOs with better MBA educations who follow riskier and more innovative business models secure superior bank performance outcomes. Such CEOs, when offered larger incentives to increase stock price volatility, or if their compensation structure contains greater equity incentives, appear able to mitigate the potentially adverse outcomes associated with excessive risk-taking and deliver significantly higher bank profitability. Taken together, CEO-specific attributes play a key role in explaining cross-sectional heterogeneity in how CEOs respond to equity incentives embedded in their compensation contracts.

Because CEOs are the primary influence on bank investment and financing decisions, CEO attitudes toward leverage could affect their bank's lending standards and financial risk levels, which can then affect a bank's sensitivity to a crisis. Ho et al. (2016) enriched the existing literature on risk-taking behaviour among banks by focusing on a managerial trait that affects banks' risk-taking: CEO overconfidence. Managerial overconfidence is an important CEO characteristic that can influence banks' risk-taking behaviours in several ways. Overconfident CEOs are those who generally think they are better than they actually are in terms of skill and judgement or in gauging the prospects of a successful outcome. Overconfident CEOs overestimate the probabilities of a positive state and the returns that will be generated by an investment project, while they underestimate the downside risks of a project and tend to choose projects with higher true risks than is optimal.[3] In the banking industry, Ho et al. (2016) showed that an overconfident CEO could relax lending standards and increase bank leverage more than the CEOs in other banks in advance of a crisis, making them more vulnerable to external shocks such as a financial crisis. During crisis years, banks with overconfident CEOs generally experienced more increases in loan defaults, greater drops in operating and stock return performance, greater increases in expected default probability, and higher likelihoods of CEO turnover or failure than other banks.

Whether or not the cultural values we inherit from our ancestors affect bank CEO decision-making is a research question addressed by a recent paper by Nguyen et al. (2018). In the impact of culture on economic outcomes, it is central to understand how a person's cultural values are formed and transmitted. Cultural attitudes adapt quickly to changes in economic incentives and opportunities. For instance, descendants of immigrants show a degree of cultural distinctiveness over several subsequent generations.[4] In the banking industry, following shocks to industry competition, banks led by CEOs who are second- or third-generation immigrants have 6.2% higher profitability than the average bank. This effect weakens over successive generations and was not detected for top executives apart from the CEO. Additional analysis attributes this effect to various prevailing cultural values in CEOs' ancestral countries. Overall, the culture of a bank CEO's ancestors influences his decision-making

[3] See Malmendier and Tate (2008) and Gervais et al. (2011).

[4] See Guiso et al. (2006) and Fernández and Fogli (2009).

behaviour, firm-related policy choices, and present performance. However, the performance effects of a certain cultural heritage depend on the market environment in which the CEO operates.

Besides these innate characteristics, heterogeneity among bank CEOs' decision-making might be influenced by characteristics acquired by CEOs while working within a bank with specific corporate governance mechanisms. We refer here to *CEO power* and *CEO turnover*. CEO power has two sources: CEO duality (Hermalin and Weisbach 1998) and internal CEO hiring (May 1995; Adams et al. 2005). CEO duality occurs when a CEO is also a chairman of the board of directors. Such a CEO can restrict information flow to other board directors and, hence, reduces the board's independent oversight of managers (Fama and Jensen 1983; Jensen 1993). Moreover, the opacity of banks, the lack of market control, and the complexity of agency costs can weaken CEO discipline, making it more important to separate leadership roles in banks (John et al. 2016). Internal hiring of a CEO may indicate that they had long-term involvement with the firm and, hence, add have 'CEO power' to influence board decisions. It follows that, as risk-averse entrenched managers, more powerful CEOs might be more risk averse and less willing to take on new business ventures than less powerful ones, which might decrease risk and increase the firm's future growth (May 1995). This view is consistent with the findings of Pathan (2009) for a sample of US banks over the period 1997–2004. More recently, Berger et al. (2016) studied the probability of bank defaults for US commercial banks over the years 2007–2010 and reported that CEO duality reduce the probability of default one year and two years prior to default. They state that in general board structure is not critical for stability, whereas managerial incentives have a highly significant and positive influence on a bank's probability of failure. Another stream of research focuses on the relationship between CEO duality and performance. Grove et al. (2011) found a negative relationship between CEO duality and bank financial performance. They showed that CEO duality affects bank performance but does not influence loan quality. These findings challenge the idea that CEO duality weakens corporate governance. Overall, CEO duality seems to strengthen bank governance from the perspectives of debtholders and society at large, as it reduces the probability of bank default and risk-taking. Yet, it might decrease the effectiveness of equity governance in banks. By analysing a sample of 378 large global banks over the period 2007–2011, Mollah and Liljeblom (2016) showed that banks with more powerful CEOs performed better during the sovereign debt crisis than during the credit crisis, despite accepting higher insolvency risk. Overall, powerful CEOs do not appear to be detrimental to performance in banking.

Risk-taking incentives for CEOs can be also provided by another corporate governance mechanism—CEO turnover decisions. Few papers have investigated the influence of CEO turnover on risk-taking incentives. The likelihood of taking risks might depend on the potential rewards, as well as the managerial consequences of poor performance. CEOs should be more inclined to take risk if there is a lower likelihood of being fired for poor performance. Moreover, as stated earlier, deregulation expands banks' growth opportunities and allows for more competition. Both effects seem likely to encourage greater risk-taking. Hayes et al. (2017) found that, after deregulation, bank CEO turnover is less sensitive to accounting performance but more sensitive to stock returns. Moreover, these changes in turnover-performance sensitivities exist only in large banks, which are best positioned to take advantage of the growth opportunities arising from deregulation, and in banks that adopt more aggressive business policies in response to deregulation. Given the fact that CEOs of large banks receive greater incentives to implement business policies that increase their organisations' exposure to risk (De Young et al. 2013; Ellul and Yerramilli 2013; Gandhi and Lustig 2015), Srivastav et al. (2017) investigated whether increases in tail risks (which measure the possibility of suffering extremely large losses), are associated with an increased likelihood of forced CEO turnover in large banks. They presented the first international study of CEO turnover in the banking industry, which was based on 261 large banks from 46 countries sampled over the 2004–2013 period. They showed that the probability of a forced CEO turnover is positively associated with idiosyncratic tail risk. This relationship strengthens with greater banking industry competition and with higher shares of inside ownership and/or subordinated debt. Overall, exposure to idiosyncratic tail risk is a valuable indicator to bank boards of the quality of CEO activity. In contrast, systematic tail risk becomes important for forced CEO turnovers only when there is a major variation in the costs of this risk to shareholders and the organisation.

3.2 CEO Compensation, Risk-Taking and Performance

Compensation practices in the banking industry are widely believed to induce excessive risk-taking and, thus, to have played an important role in causing the recent financial crisis (e.g., Bebchuk and Spamann 2010; IMF 2010; Board of Governors et al. 2010). The question of whether compensation policies are structured to promote risk-taking in order to maximise the value of the put option feature of fixed-rate deposit insurance has attracted considerable interest from bank regulators and academics. One of the early studies on CEO compensation in the banking industry is that of Houston and James (1995). They found that compensation policies in banking are not designed to promote excessive risk-taking. However, they showed that, compared with CEOs in other industries, CEOs in US banks, on average, receive less cash compensation, hold fewer stock options, and receive a smaller percentage of their total compensation in the form of options and stocks (over the period 1980–1990). Differences in the compensation structures of banks and non-banks, as well as within the banking industry generally, can be explained by the nature of the firm's set of assets and investment opportunities, which has a profound influence on the type of agency problems that a particular firm faces. Their results provide support to the 'contracting hypothesis'. Adams and Mehran (2003) confirmed this trend for a sample of US bank over the period 1986–1996. They stated that, in the last few years, the use of stock options in banking executive compensation packages has increased. Although this pattern has followed the pattern of other industries, the growth and level of stock options remain significantly lower in banks than in manufacturing firms. Similarly, other studies show a significant difference in the levels and structures of executive compensation between banks and non-financial companies, both in the US and abroad (Becher et al. 2005; Gregg et al. 2012). The pronounced reliance on long-term compensation for the highest-paid employees indicates that employee retention matters (Oyer 2004), as long-term compensation emerges in optimal contracts to lengthen employees' view on their tenure at the current employer (Holmstrom and Joan Ricart 1986; Giannetti 2011). Moreover, theories that stress the importance of competition for talent (e.g., Gabaix and Landier 2008; Terviö 2008) have recently been supported by Giannetti and Metzger (2015). They examine a sample of 531 individuals located in 23 countries between 1996 and 2012. They confirm that a positive correlation exists between the level of pay and the amount of long-term compensation offered in the financial industry, not only for CEOs, but also for non-executive employees below top management (another profession characterised by high competition for talent). In financial centres, this evidence appears stronger, indicating that retention motives are important drivers of the level and structure of compensation offered to high-talent employees.

An important channel through which we observe an increase of sensitivity of CEO compensation to bank performance is through changes in the regulatory environment. In a principal-agent framework, firms may alter the structure of the incentive contracts they offer to their executives in response to changing product market competition (Schmidt 1997; Raith 2003; Scharfstein 1988; Hermalin 1992). Competitive environments generate implicit incentives that determine the design of compensation packages and, hence, alter the need and magnitude of explicit incentives. Under the managerial talent hypothesis, markets that are more competitive require managers with greater skills and/or talent. Accordingly, a higher level of pay is required to attract more skilled/talented managers to more competitive environments. Moreover, CEOs in less-regulated environments will have payment contracts with a more significant component of performance-based pay, such as stock options. Moreover, with the expansion of managerial discretion following bank deregulation, an expansion of the investment risk-return opportunity set is also relevant. Performance-based pay schemes tied to shareholder returns encourage bank CEOs to search out and invest in these positive NPV projects. Greater growth opportunities are associated with a stronger pay-performance relationship (according to the contracting hypothesis). Furthermore, a risk-averse CEO should demand a pay premium for accepting the increased risk of equity-based pay (Edmans and Gabaix 2011).

Several papers have studied the effect that deregulation has on bank CEOs' compensation level and structure. In the context of the banking industry, and particularly in the US, regulatory reforms in the 1980s and 1990s created a more competitive environment. This expanded managerial discretion and investment opportunities but, at the same time, put pressure on CEOs to perform in more competitive banking markets. In the US, the banking industry underwent two major phases of deregulation in the 1990s: the *Riegle-Neal Interstate and Branching Efficiency Act* in 1994 and the *Gramm-Leach-Bliley Act* in 1999. Both Acts provided US commercial banks with greater growth opportunities through the expansion of operating branches in different states (i.e., elimination of interstate banking), and with diversification opportunities via entering the insurance and investment banking fields. Following these changes, CEO compensation structures exhibited a shift towards having more stock-option components during the period over which an expanded investment opportunity set exists because of regulatory changes.

By comparing the pay-performance sensitivity of CEOs before and after the introduction of interstate regulations in the 1980s, Hubbard and Palia (1995) and Crawford et al. (1995) provided strong evidence of increased pay-performance sensitivity after deregulation. Further, the increases in pay-performance sensitivities were not clustered in low-capital banks but affected high-capital banks as well, confirming both the managerial talent hypothesis and the contracting hypothesis. In other words, the marked increase in the sensitivity of bank CEO pay for performance was attributed to deregulation and not to enhanced risk-taking incentives arising from the decline in bank capital that occurred during the 1980s. Collins et al. (1995) further showed that total compensation, and the incentive to total compensation ratio, increased substantially as financial innovation and deregulation during the 1980s created growth opportunities for banking organisations. Interestingly, CEO pay-performance sensitivity differs between investment and commercial banks. Fields and Fraser (1999) found that pay-performance sensitivity at investment banks was quite high and that the entry of commercial banks into investment banking (through the relaxation of Section 20 subsidiaries) had only a very limited effect on the pay-performance sensitivity of their CEOs. Pay-performance sensitivities for commercial banks beginning securities underwriting, and for commercial banks that have chosen not to enter investment banking, are similar and are both lower than for investment banks. By using a sample of 68 banks involving 70 CEOs over the period from 1992 to 2000, Chen et al. (2006) explicitly examined the impact of option-based compensation on several market-based measures of bank risk. They showed that following the deregulation of the 1990s (i.e., the *Riegle-Neal Interstate and Branching Efficiency Act* in 1994 and the *Gramm-Leach-Bliley Act* in 1999), banks increasingly employed stock option-based compensation and, as a result, the structure of executive compensation induced risk-taking. Their findings support the theoretical arguments presented by John et al. (2000), who suggested that regulators need to consider a new paradigm that explicitly provides the appropriate incentives/disincentives for risk-taking within compensation structures. They suggested that regulatory oversight of the compensation structures employed in the banking industry is therefore important. Similarly, Cuñat and Guadalupe (2009) study supported this evidence by clarifying the role of deregulation in increasing banking competition. Higher competition affected the structure of pay compensation (but not the level) and reduced the fixed component of pay while increasing performance-related pay (higher sensitivity of stock option grants).[5]

Recent failures of large financial institutions have been blamed on giving CEO incentives to take excessive risks (Bebchuk and Spamann 2010; Bebchuk et al. 2010), which again highlights the need to deeply investigate how such incentives would

[5]This evidence was found for the sensitivity of both total compensation and stock option grants to bank performance.

emerge in equilibrium. In fact, payments in the banking industry rose tremendously in the decade leading up to the 2007–08 financial crises, triggering intensive debates on the optimal level and structure of compensation schemes. Did corporate governance fail? Or on the contrary, are bank shareholders inherently biased toward excessive risk-taking and consequently setting CEO incentives too high? This implies that the observed incentives of bank CEOs to take excessive risks can be viewed as a manifestation of shareholder power rather than as a failure of corporate governance. This, in turn, calls for regulatory intervention. In the US, Section 956 of the 2010 *Dodd-Frank Act* requires that banking agencies regulate compensation arrangements at large financial institutions to discourage inappropriate risk-taking. In 2011 and 2016, the agencies proposed rules to regulate pay in financial institutions.[6] Outside of the USA, regulatory action has also been intense. The European Union approved directives CRD III (in 2010) and CRD IV (in 2013), which contain provisions that regulate compensation at financial institutions. CRD IV (Directive 2013/36/EU, Art. 94(m)), introduced regulatory requirements to defer compensation in the European bank regulatory framework. The Committee of European Banking Supervisors (in 2010) and the European Banking Authority (in 2015) issued guidelines on sound remuneration policies. In the UK, the Financial Services Authority issued in 2009, and amended in 2010, the so-called *Remuneration Code*, and the Prudential Regulation Authority and Financial Conduct Authority issued remuneration rules for financial firms in 2015. At the multinational level, the Financial Stability Forum issued the *Principles for Sound Compensation Practices* in 2009.

Despite the attention devoted to executive pay by regulators, empirical research provides mixed support for the hypothesis that CEO compensation in the run-up to the crisis influenced bank risk-taking. The financial crisis has been used as a case study to test whether the ex-ante incentives in executive compensation contracts are associated with ex-post risk-taking, and whether bank boards of directors materially attempt to mitigate or moderate ex-post risk-taking by readjusting the incentive structures in executive pay packages.

In particular, there appears to be an emerging policy consensus in the US and Europe that bonus payments, in particular, have promoted excessive risk-taking in the financial sector. For instance, the Financial Stability Board (2009) concluded in a report for the Group of Twenty that "high short-term profits led to generous bonus payments to employees [which] amplified the excessive risk-taking that severely threatened the global financial system" (p. 3). In response, US compensation guidelines for CEOs and other senior executives at large banks come close to dictating that bonuses be paid in equity-based instruments, that payments be deferred, and that vesting be performance-contingent (Boards of Governors 2011, p. 33). Similarly, the Committee of European Banking Supervisors (2010) proposes in its draft guidelines on remuneration policies that at least 50% of variable compensation (including bonus

[6]Recent regulatory proposals in the USA also contain requirements to defer compensation (OCC, Board, FDIC, FHFA, NCUA, and SEC, 2016, §7). Compensation regulation proposals that do not require deferred compensation instead rely on forward-looking risk measures, such as CDS spreads, to reduce risk shifting.

payments) should be non-cash. CEO bonuses are an important component of executive pay but the effect of bonus payments on managerial risk preferences is likely to differ from that exerted by option grants.

Since the payoffs from option holdings are convex functions of the volatility of stock returns, options incentivise CEOs to increase the volatility of share prices by engaging in riskier activities. In contrast, CEO bonus plans do not provide convex payoffs (Smith and Stulz 1985) and may not promote excessive risk-taking (Noe et al. 1996) for earnings performance exceeding the thresholds at which bonus payments become payable. Vallascas and Hagendorff (2013) demonstrate the bright side of bonus payments and cautioned regulators about attempting to regulate bonus pay. For a sample of 76 US and 41 European banks over the period 2000–2008, they showed that increases in CEO cash bonuses lower the default risk of banks, except for financially distressed banks seeking to maximise the value of the financial safety net, or when banks operate under weak bank regulatory regimes. Second, since bonuses are linked to higher bank risk-taking at the riskiest banks, risk-shifting incentives at these institutions are only likely to be constrained if compensation practices more closely align the interests of managers and debtholders. It follows that when banks are highly risky, regulatory interference is the preferred alternative to greater shareholder-oriented pay setting (e.g., giving shareholders a vote on compensation policy—"say on pay"—as championed by the *Dodd-Frank Act*; Zalewska 2016).

Bannier et al. (2013) showed that bonuses increase competition for bank employees, thereby confirming the impact of competitive pressure on remuneration schemes as claimed by many industry representatives. They found that in equilibrium, only high-ability workers receive bonuses, and excessive risk-taking is deliberately accepted in order to reduce low-ability workers' information rents. Their model suggests that legal restrictions on bonuses would increase profits and welfare at the same time. This assigns a generally positive role to regulatory interventions: restricting bonus compensation may help to settle on a more efficient structure of fixed and performance-related payments by reducing excessive risk-taking.

To achieve this, Hakenes and Schnabel (2014) discussed the use of a bonus cap to curb risk-taking incentives while considering agency problems, safety nets (especially for SIFIs) and CEO compensation. They support the view that it is optimal for a welfare-maximising regulator to impose caps on bank bonuses, while raising liabilities can be counterproductive. If the bonus cap makes compensation less sensitive to bank performance, this is the opposite of what is desirable in an incentive-compensation plan. Alternatively, Bolton et al. (2015) proposed that a linear adjustment to credit risk (by linking pay to the premium on credit default swaps) should be added to equity-based pay to mitigate the incentives a bank executive has to risk-shift onto taxpayers. Jensen and Meckling (1976) argued that if a CEO holds more wealth in the form of inside equity, then their interests are aligned with those of shareholders, which causes more risk-taking. On the other hand, if a CEO holds more wealth in the form of inside debt (pensions and deferred compensation), then they will care more about the long-term solvency of the firm.[7] Similarly, Edmans and Liu (2011) argue that increasing the share of deferred compensation and other debt-like forms of executive pay will turn executives into unsecured bondholders with a financial interest in the liquidation value of a firm and, thus, remedy incentives for CEOs to shift risk.[8] This structure aligns the incentives of managers with debtholders, thereby deterring managers from risk-shifting decisions.[9]

Inspired by these insights, Bennett et al. (2015) analysed inside debt (i.e., pension benefits and deferred compensation) and found that higher pre-crisis holdings of inside debt relative to inside equity by a CEO, after controlling for firm leverage, was associated with lower default risk and better performance during the crisis period. In other words, they found a negative relationship between bank CEOs' debt-like compensation (inside debt) and bank risk during the financial crisis. However, these results cannot be generalised to all type of banks, as Thanassoulis and Tanaka (2018) found that, in the case of Too Big To Fail (TBTF) banks, paying executives partly in debt fails to mitigate project choice distortion when debt markets are informed. In contrast, clawback rules and linking pay to interest rates can both incentivise executives to make socially-optimal risk choices, but only if they are accompanied by appropriate restrictions on the curvature of pay with respect to the bank's market value.

Certainly, to reduce risk shifting, a regulator can constrain the compensation of CEOs and other bank managers. However, the governance structure is likely to adapt in order to preserve shareholders' interests. Kolm et al. (2016) discussed how boards might become more active when regulators constrain CEO compensation, and the implications of having an active board combined with regulation of bank capital and CEO compensation. They show that with an active board, combining regulation of bank capital and CEO compensation is more efficient than using either of the two tools in isolation. Requiring CEO compensation that is linear in total bank value curtails CEOs' willingness to participate in risk shifting, while a higher regulatory capital requirement reduces the positive effect of risk shifting on shareholder value. The former prevents CEOs proposing strategies that result in inefficiently high risk, while the latter ensures that a shareholder-friendly board is willing to accept a larger set of strategies that reduce risk.

In addition to the research reviewed above, other studies have tested whether such risk-taking manifests itself in bank performance. These have provided contradictory findings. Some papers support Bebchuk et al. (2010) findings. For instance, Bai and

---

[7]Ferrarini (2015) discusses recent international rules concerning the mandatory structure of managerial compensation in banks. He questions the idea that managerial compensation has led banks to take excessive risks during the financial crisis and suggests an improvement in capital adequacy and organisational requirements rather than a direct intervention in bankers' incentives.

[8]A different strand of the literature focuses on the inefficiencies that arise in the labour market for bank CEOs (Thanassoulis 2012; Bannier et al. 2013; Archarya et al. 2016). In these models, labour market imperfections lead to risk-taking incentives that are excessive from the bank's perspective, which provides a rationale for regulation.

[9]Sundaram and Yermack (2007) and Gerakos (2010) empirically tested Jensen and Meckling (1976) insight on CEOs of non-financial firms.

Elyasiani (2013) found that higher CEO vegas[10] lead to greater bank instability (measured by Z-scores), and that the association between bank stability and managerial compensation is bi-directional: higher vegas induce greater risk and vice versa. They also found that the risk incentives of CEOs in large banks are much greater than those of CEOs in small banks, posing a threat to the stability of the financial industry and the overall economic system. In the same vein, Bhagat and Bolton (2014) showed that incentives generated by executive compensation programs are positively correlated with excessive risk-taking by banks. Their evidence led them to recommend that executive incentive compensation should only consist of restricted stock and restricted stock options—restricted in the sense that the executive cannot sell the shares or exercise the options for two to four years after leaving the bank. This type of structure will more appropriately align the long-term incentives of senior executives with the interests of the stockholders. The above incentive compensation proposal was developed and detailed in Bhagat and Romano (2010) and Bhagat et al. (2014), and is consistent with theoretical papers which suggest that a significant component of incentive compensation should consist of stock and stock options with long vesting periods (see Edmans et al. 2009; Peng and Röell 2014). Gande and Kalpathy (2017) provide evidence that vegas before a crisis are positively associated with the amount of US Federal Reserve emergency loans provided to banks. They used this as an ex-post measure of bank risk, suggesting that future policy work should focus on the attributes of financial CEO pay and compensation structures to curb excessive risk-taking, such as by incorporating the incentive features of CEO compensation (e.g., CEO vegas) into the pricing of FDIC insurance (John et al. 2000). A positive relationship between termination payments and bank risk was found by Brown et al. (2015), providing further empirical evidence on executive compensation and risk-taking.

On the other hand, Fahlenbrach and Stulz (2011) found no relationship between pre-crisis CEO vegas and crisis-period bank performance measures. They concluded that the poor performance of these banks during the crisis was attributable to an extremely negative realisation of the high-risk nature of their investment and trading strategies. A plausible explanation for these findings is that CEOs focused on the interests of their shareholders in the build-up to the crisis and took actions that they believed the market would welcome. Ex-post, these actions were costly to their banks and to themselves when the results turned out to be poor. These poor results were not expected by the CEOs to the extent that they did not reduce or hedge their holdings of shares in anticipation of a poor outcome. The authors also ruled out the possibility that the incentive effects of compensation policies were no different in two subsamples of Troubled Asset Relief Program (TARP) and no-TARP recipients. Boyallian and Ruiz-Verdú (2017) found that in a sample of large US financial firms, a higher pre-crisis sensitivity of a CEO's wealth to his firm's stock price (delta), was associated with a significantly higher probability of failure during the 2007–10 financial crisis in highly levered firms, but not in less-levered firms. In line with the

[10]Vega measures the change in CEO wealth associated with a 1% change in a bank's stock return volatility. This measure is also labelled the 'risk-sensitivity of compensation'.

findings of Fahlenbrach and Stulz (2011), they found no significant relationship between bank failure and the sensitivity of the value of CEOs' stock option portfolios to the volatility of their firms' stock (vega). Thus, a better alignment between CEO and shareholder incentives seems to have encouraged CEOs to shift risk to debtholders and depositors, but the sign and strength of those incentives depend on bank leverage. These results imply that banking supervisors should consider compensation arrangements in relation to leverage when they evaluate the risk-taking incentives created by executive compensation. Their results differ from those of Bennett et al. (2015), who found a negative relationship between inside debt and bank risk by estimating the residual effect of compensation incentives after controlling for a large battery of variables.

De Young et al. (2013) provided mixed evidence for small and large banks. They found that ex-ante executive compensation in financial firms after the deregulation of 1999 encouraged increased risk-taking, as indicated by higher levels of credit risk, fee income from non-traditional services, and private mortgage securitisations. However, ex-post, bank boards adjusted CEO risk-taking incentives in a manner consistent with mitigation or moderation of higher than average levels of risk-taking. This feedback effect, however, was absent for the very largest banks with strong growth opportunities and a history of highly aggressive risk-taking incentives.

3.3 CEO Compensation and Corporate Policies

The relationship between management compensation and firm size has a long and consistent record of empirical validity.[11] Furthermore, as we have seen in the previous Sect. 3.2, the connection between pay and performance is also well documented. Merger and acquisition (M&A) decisions significantly affect both. Moreover, M&As are one of the most important resource allocation decisions made by CEOs. Given these interrelationships between pay, performance and size, some research papers have examined whether M&As increase CEO compensation and whether compensation structures affect CEOs' decisions to acquire other firms. This suggests that CEOs may take compensation into account when considering strategic decisions such as mergers. The seminal work by Bliss and Rosen (2001) analysed a sample of 32 of the US's largest banks over the period 1986–1995. They showed that M&As significantly increase CEO compensation, even after accounting for typical announcement date stock price declines, mainly via the effect of size on compensation. Compensation structures affected M&A decisions, since CEOs with more stock-based compensation were less likely to make an acquisition. Minnick et al. (2011) extended the findings of Bliss and Rosen (2001) by studying a sample of 159 mergers of publicly-traded bank holding companies from 1991 to 2005. They showed how pay-for-performance sensitivity in executive compensation affected the acquired stocks' returns close to merger announcements, the probability of acquisition ex-ante, and changes in

[11] See Ciscel and Carroll (1980) and Agarwal (1981), among others.

operating performance after acquisitions. Differently from Bliss and Rosen (2001), they showed that the more closely a bank CEO's wealth is tied to the bank's stock, the more consistent acquisition decisions are with shareholder value maximisation. Specifically, when CEOs are paid for performance, they are less likely to make acquisitions that do not create shareholder value and are more likely to seek out value-enhancing investments. Following acquisitions, banks with CEOs paid for performance experience greater improvements in operating performance. However, the effect of pay-for-performance sensitivity is only evident in small and medium-sized banks and is absent in large banks. Given the fact that M&As are clearly investment strategies, one can relate changes in bank risk following a deal to CEO risk-taking incentives. Hagendorff and Vallascas (2011) focused on CEO vegas in relation to the risks of bank mergers by examining whether a causal relationship existed between CEO pay and risk-taking in the banking sector following M&A transactions. Using a sample of 172 US bank mergers over the period 1993–2007, they showed that CEOs with higher pay-risk sensitivities engaged in risk-inducing mergers. The findings were driven by two types of acquisitions: those completed after bank deregulation (that had expanded banks' risk-taking opportunities) and those completed by the largest banks (where shareholders benefit from 'too big to fail' support by regulators and gain most by shifting risk to other stakeholders). Once again, these results confirm the view that the incentive structure of CEO compensation has implications for financial stability, because high-vega CEOs make investment choices that increase the default risk of their institutions. These finding support the belief in regulating CEO pay in the banking industry by, for instance, imposing limits on the amount of risk-inducing compensation, linking capital requirements or deposit insurance premiums to risk-taking incentives, or increasing the amount of deferred compensation. This rules out the idea that increased shareholder involvement in setting executive compensation (for instance, by giving them a vote on "say on pay" compensation policy) would mitigate risk-taking in the banking industry.

The banking literature also offers a contribution to research on CEO power and bank dividend policies. Onali et al. (2016) used a sample of 109 European-listed banks over the period 2005–2013. However, banking dividend policy is an under-researched area. Abreu and Gulamhussen (2013) showed that, in determining bank dividend policy both before and during the financial crisis, bank size, profitability, growth opportunities, and agency cost play major roles. While monitoring in non-financial firms comes from outside shareholders, in banks it also comes from government. It is clear that there exists a conflict of interest between the government and outside shareholders. Typically, the government has a preference for low bank pay-outs, whereas outside shareholders prefer higher pay-outs. In fact, governments have incentives to monitor bank dividend policy so as to minimise the probability that excessive dividend payouts lead to inadequate equity capital buffers. For this reason, restrictions on dividend payments and share repurchases for under-capitalised banks are part of the Basel III framework. All other things being equal, a low dividend payout ratio can reduce the strength of government monitoring of CEOs, because of its positive impact on bank stability. A low dividend payout ratio could reduce potential losses for the deposit insurance provider, and in the case of a capital shortfall, the government is incentivised to exert monitoring pressure on the bank. In the managerial entrenchment literature, dividend payout ratios are positively related to CEO power, since dividends discourage monitoring from minority shareholders. In the banking industry, bank CEOs stay between regulators and shareholders and should make decisions on the levels of dividend payouts. Such decisions depend on whether entrenched CEOs wish to discourage monitoring from the government (entrenched CEOs prefer low dividend payout ratios), or from outside shareholders (entrenched CEOs prefer high dividend payout ratios). Onali et al. (2016) found that monitoring by the government leads to an inverse relationship between CEO power and dividend payouts. Entrenched bank CEOs pay lower dividends and, in doing so, are less likely to attract undesired attention from government regulators. Moreover, negative relationships between CEO ownership, CEO tenure, and payout ratios were found, while a positive link between unforced CEO turnover events and dividend payout ratios was found. CEO ownership and CEO tenure are also negatively related to bank performance, while unforced CEO turnover events are associated with increases in bank performance. These findings suggest that entrenched CEOs in European banks do not have an incentive to increase payout ratios to discourage monitoring from shareholders. Overall, these results are consistent with the view that, in banking, entrenched CEOs do not have strong incentives to pay large dividends, because of a combination of weak minority shareholder regulation, an inefficient market for corporate control, and concerns of the government over bank soundness. These factors lead to a negative relationship between CEO power and dividend payouts.

References

Abreu, J.F., and M.A. Gulamhussen. 2013. Dividend payouts: Evidence from US bank holding companies in the context of the financial crisis. *Journal of Corporate Finance* 22: 54–65.

Acharya, V., Pagano, M., and P. Volpin. 2016. Seeking alpha: Excess risk taking and competition for managerial talent. *Review of Financial Studies* 29 (10): 2565–2599.

Adams, R.B., and H. Mehran. 2003. Is corporate governance different for bank holding companies? Available at SSRN 387561.

Adams, R.B., H. Almeida, and D. Ferreira. 2005. Powerful CEOs and their impact on corporate performance. *The Review of Financial Studies* 18 (4): 1403–1432.

Agarwal, N.C. 1981. Determinants of executive compensation. *Industrial Relations: A Journal of Economy and Society* 20 (1): 36–45.

Bai, G., and E. Elyasiani. 2013. Bank stability and managerial compensation. *Journal of Banking & Finance* 37 (3): 799–813.

Bannier, C.E., E. Feess, and N. Packham. 2013. Competition, bonuses, and risk-taking in the banking industry. *Review of Finance* 17 (2): 653–690.

Bebchuk, L.A., and H. Spamann. 2010. Regulating bankers' pay. *Georgetown Law Journal* 98 (2): 247–287.

Bebchuk, L.A., A. Cohen, and H. Spamann. 2010. The wages of failure: Executive compensation at Bear Stearns and Lehman 2000–2008. *Yale Journal on Regulation* 27: 257.

Beber, A., and D. Fabbri. 2012. Who times the foreign exchange market? Corporate speculation and CEO characteristics. *Journal of Corporate Finance* 18 (5): 1065–1087.

Becher, D.A., T.L. Campbell II, and M.B. Frye. 2005. Incentive compensation for bank directors: The impact of deregulation. *The journal of business* 78 (5): 1753–1778.

Bennett, R.L., L. Güntay, and H. Unal. 2015. Inside debt, bank default risk, and performance during the crisis. *Journal of Financial Intermediation* 24 (4): 487–513.

Berger, A.N., B. Imbierowicz, and C. Rauch. 2016. The roles of corporate governance in bank failures during the recent financial crisis. *Journal of Money, Credit and Banking* 48 (4): 729–770.

Bertrand, M., and A. Schoar. 2003. Managing with style: The effect of managers on firm policies. *The Quarterly Journal of Economics* 118 (4): 1169–1208.

Bhagat, S., and B. Bolton. 2014. Financial crisis and bank executive incentive compensation. *Journal of Corporate Finance* 25: 313–341.

Bhagat, S., and R. Romano. 2010. Reforming executive compensation: Simplicity, transparency and committing to the long-term. *European Company and Financial Law Review* 7 (2): 273–296.

Bhagat, S., B. Bolton, and R. Romano. 2014. Getting incentives right: is deferred bank executive compensation sufficient. *Yale Journal on Regulation* 31: 523.

Bliss, R.T., and R.J. Rosen. 2001. CEO compensation and bank mergers. *Journal of Financial Economics* 61 (1): 107–138.

Financial Stability Board. 2009. *Principles for Sound Compensation Practices*. Basel, Switzerland.

Board of Governors of the Federal Reserve System, Federal Deposit Insurance Corporation, Office of the Comptroller of the Currency, treasury and Office of Thrift Supervision. 2010. Guidance on Sound Incentive Compensation Policies.

Bolton, P., H. Mehran, and J. Shapiro. 2015. Executive compensation and risk taking. *Review of Finance* 19 (6): 2139–2181.

Boyallian, P., and P. Ruiz-Verdú. 2017. Leverage, CEO risk-taking incentives, and bank failure during the 2007–2010 financial crisis. *Review of Finance* 1: 43.

Brown, K., R. Jha, and P. Pacharn. 2015. Ex ante CEO severance pay and risk-taking in the financial services sector. *Journal of Banking & Finance* 59: 111–126.

Chen, C.R., T.L. Steiner, and A.M. Whyte. 2006. Does stock option-based executive compensation induce risk-taking? An analysis of the banking industry. *Journal of Banking & Finance* 30 (3): 915–945.

Ciscel, D.H., and T.M. Carroll. 1980. The determinants of executive salaries: An econometric survey. *The Review of Economics and Statistics* 62 (1): 7–13.

Collins, M.C., D.W. Blackwell, and J.F. Sinkey. 1995. The relationship between corporate compensation policies and investment opportunities: Empirical evidence for large bank holding companies. *Financial Management* 24 (3): 40–53.

Committee of European Banking Supervisors. 2010. Consultation paper on guidelines on remuneration policies and practices. http://www.eba.europa.eu/documents/10180/16094/CP42.pdf.

Crawford, A.J., J.R. Ezzell, and J.A. Miles. 1995. Bank CEO pay-performance relations and the effects of deregulation. *Journal of Business* 68 (2): 231–256.

Cuñat, V., and M. Guadalupe. 2009. Executive compensation and competition in the banking and financial sectors. *Journal of Banking & Finance* 33 (3): 495–504.

Custódio, C., and D. Metzger. 2013. How do CEOs matter? The effect of industry expertise on acquisition returns. *The Review of Financial Studies* 26 (8): 2008–2047.

Custódio, C., M.A. Ferreira, and P. Matos. 2013. Generalists versus specialists: Lifetime work experience and chief executive officer pay. *Journal of Financial Economics* 108 (2): 471–492.

De Young, R., E.Y. Peng, and M. Yan. 2013. Executive compensation and business policy choices at U.S. commercial banks. *Journal of Financial and Quantitative Analysis* 48 (1): 165–196.

Edmans, A., X. Gabaix, T. Sadzik, and Y. Sannikov. 2009. *Dynamic incentive accounts*. National Bureau of Economic Research.

Edmans, A., and X. Gabaix. 2011. The effect of risk on the CEO market. *The Review of Financial Studies* 24 (8): 2822–2863.

Edmans, A., and Q. Liu. 2011. Inside debt. *Review of Finance* 15 (1): 75–102.

Ellul, A., and V. Yerramilli. 2013. Stronger risk controls, lower risk: Evidence from US bank holding companies. *The Journal of Finance* 68 (5): 1757–1803.

Fahlenbrach, R., and R.M. 2011. Bank CEO incentives and the credit crisis. *Journal of Financial Economics* 99 (1): 11–26.

Fama, E., and M.C. Jensen. 1983. Separation of ownership and control. *Journal of Law and Economics* 26: 1983a.

Fee, C.E., C.J. Hadlock, and J.R. Pierce. 2013. Managers with and without style: Evidence using exogenous variation. *The Review of Financial Studies* 26 (3): 567–601.

Fernández, R., and A. Fogli. 2009. Culture: An empirical investigation of beliefs, work, and fertility. *American Economic Journal: Macroeconomics* 1 (1): 146–177.

Ferrarini, G. 2015. CRD IV and the mandatory structure of bankers' pay. CGI Law Working Paper No. 289.

Fields, L.P., and D.R. Fraser. 1999. On the compensation implications of commercial bank entry into investment banking. *Journal of Banking & Finance* 23 (8): 1261–1276.

Frydman, C. 2007. Rising through the ranks. The evolution of the market for corporate executives 1936–2003. MIT Working Paper.

Gabaix, X., and A. Landier. 2008. Why has CEO pay increased so much? *The Quarterly Journal of Economics* 123 (1): 49–100.

Gande, A., and S. Kalpathy. 2017. CEO compensation and risk-taking at financial firms: Evidence from U.S. federal loan assistance. *Journal of Corporate Finance* 47 (Supplement C): 131–150.

Gandhi, P., and H. Lustig. 2015. Size anomalies in US bank stock returns. *The Journal of Finance* 70 (2): 733–768.

Gerakos, J. 2010. Chief executive officers and the pay–pension tradeoff. *Journal of Pension Economics & Finance* 9 (2): 303–319.

Gervais, S., J.B. Heaton, and T. Odean. 2011. Overconfidence, compensation contracts, and capital budgeting. *The Journal of Finance* 66 (5): 1735–1777.

Giannetti, M. 2011. Serial CEO incentives and the structure of managerial contracts. *Journal of Financial Intermediation* 20 (4): 633–662.

Giannetti, M., and D. Metzger. 2015. Compensation and competition for talent: Evidence from the financial industry. *Finance Research Letters* 12: 11–16.

Governors, B.O. 2011. *Guidance on sound incentive compensation policies*. Federal Reserve System.

Graham, J.R., C.R. Harvey, and M. Puri. 2013. Managerial attitudes and corporate actions. *Journal of Financial Economics* 109 (1): 103–121.

Gregg, P., S. Jewell, and I. Tonks. 2012. Executive pay and performance: Did bankers' bonuses cause the crisis? *International Review of Finance* 12 (1): 89–122.

Grove, H., L. Patelli, L.M. Victoravich, and P.T. Xu. 2011. Corporate governance and performance in the wake of the financial crisis: Evidence from US commercial banks. *Corporate Governance: An International Review* 19 (5): 418–436.

Guiso, L., P. Sapienza, and L. Zingales. 2006. Does culture affect economic outcomes? *The Journal of Economic Perspectives* 20 (2): 23–48.

Hagendorff, J., and F. Vallascas. 2011. CEO pay incentives and risk-taking: Evidence from bank acquisitions. *Journal of Corporate Finance* 17 (4): 1078–1095.

Hakenes, H., and I. Schnabel. 2014. Bank bonuses and bailouts. *Journal of Money, Credit and Banking* 46 (s1): 259–288.

Hambrick, D.C., and P.A. Mason. 1984. upper Echelons: The organization as a reflection of its top managers. *The Academy of Management Review* 9 (2): 193–206.

Hayes, R.M., X.S. Tian, and X. Wang. 2017. *Banking industry deregulation and CEO incentives*. Evidence from Bank CEO Turnover.

Hermalin, B.E. 1992. The effects of competition on executive behavior. *The RAND Journal of Economics* 23 (3): 350–365.

Hermalin, B.E., and M.S. Weisbach. 1998. Endogenously chosen boards of directors and their monitoring of the CEO. *The American Economic Review* 88 (1): 96–118.

Ho, P.-H., C.-W. Huang, C.-Y. Lin, and J.-F. Yen. 2016. CEO overconfidence and financial crisis: Evidence from bank lending and leverage. *Journal of Financial Economics* 120 (1): 194–209.

Holmstrom, B., and I.C. Joan Ricart. 1986. Managerial incentives and capital management. *The Quarterly Journal of Economics* 101 (4): 835–860.

Houston, J.F., and C. James. 1995. CEO compensation and bank risk. Is compensation in banking structured to promote risk taking? *Journal of monetary Economics* 36 (2): 405–431.

Hubbard, R.G., and D. Palia. 1995. Executive pay and performance Evidence from the U.S. banking industry. *Journal of Financial Economics* 39 (1): 105–130.

IMF. 2010. A fair and substantial contribution by the financial sector. Report for the G-20, International Monetary Fund, Washington, DC.

Jensen, M.C. 1993. The modern industrial revolution, exit, and the failure of internal control systems. *The Journal of Finance* 48 (3): 831–880.

Jensen, M.C., and W.H. Meckling. 1976. Theory of the firm: Managerial behavior, agency costs and ownership structure. *Journal of Financial Economics* 3 (4): 305–360.

John, K., A. Saunders, and L.W. Senbet. 2000. A theory of bank regulation and management compensation. *Review of Financial Studies* 13 (1): 95–125.

John, K., S. De Masi, and A. Paci. 2016. Corporate governance in banks. *Corporate Governance: An International Review* 24 (3): 303–321.

Kaplan, S.N., M.M. Klebanov, and M. Sorensen. 2012. Which CEO characteristics and abilities matter? *The Journal of Finance* 67 (3): 973–1007.

King, T., A. Srivastav, and J. Williams. 2016. What's in an education? Implications of CEO education for bank performance. *Journal of Corporate Finance* 37: 287–308.

Kolm, J., C. Laux, and G. Lóránth. 2016. Bank regulation, CEO compensation, and boards. *Review of Finance*, rfw046.

Malmendier, U., and G. Tate. 2005. CEO overconfidence and corporate investment. *Journal of Finance* 60 (6): 2661–2700.

Malmendier, U., and G. Tate. 2008. Who makes acquisitions? CEO overconfidence and the market's reaction. *Journal of Financial Economics* 89 (1): 20–43.

May, D.O. 1995. Do managerial motives influence firm risk reduction strategies? *The Journal of Finance* 50 (4): 1291–1308.

Minnick, K., H. Unal, and L. Yang. 2011. Pay for performance? CEO compensation and acquirer returns in BHCs. *The Review of Financial Studies* 24 (2): 439–472.

Mollah, S., and E. Liljeblom. 2016. Governance and bank characteristics in the credit and sovereign debt crises—The impact of CEO power1. *Journal of Financial Stability* 27: 59–73.

Nguyen, D.D.L., J. Hagendorff, and A. Eshraghi. 2015. Which executive characteristics create value in banking? Evidence from appointment announcements. *Corporate Governance: An International Review* 23 (2): 112–128.

Nguyen, D.D., J. Hagendorff, and A. Eshraghi. 2018. Does a CEO's cultural heritage affect performance under competitive pressure? *The Review of Financial Studies* 31 (1): 97–141.

Noe, T.H., M.J. Rebello, and L.D. Wall. 1996. Managerial rents and regulatory intervention in troubled banks. *Journal of Banking & Finance* 20 (2): 331–350.

Onali, E., R. Galiakhmetova, P. Molyneux, and G. Torluccio. 2016. CEO power, government monitoring, and bank dividends. *Journal of Financial Intermediation* 27: 89–117.

Oyer, P. 2004. Why do firms use incentives that have no incentive effects? *The Journal of Finance* 59 (4): 1619–1650.

Pathan, S. 2009. Strong boards, CEO power and bank risk-taking. *Journal of Banking & Finance* 33 (7): 1340–1350.

Peng, L., and A. Röell. 2014. Managerial incentives and stock price manipulation. *The Journal of Finance* 69 (2): 487–526.

Raith, M. 2003. Competition, risk, and managerial incentives. *American Economic Review* 93 (4): 1425–1436.

Scharfstein, D. 1988. Product-market competition and managerial slack. *The RAND Journal of Economics* 19 (1):147–155.

Schmidt, K.M. 1997. Managerial incentives and product market competition. *The Review of Economic Studies* 64 (2): 191–213.

Smith, C.W., and R.M. Stulz. 1985. The determinants of firms' hedging policies. *The Journal of Financial and Quantitative Analysis* 20 (4): 391–405.

Srivastav, A., K. Keasey, S. Mollah, and F. Vallascas. 2017. CEO turnover in large banks: Does tail risk matter? *Journal of Accounting and Economics* 64 (1): 37–55.
Sundaram, R.K., and D.L. Yermack. 2007. Pay me later: Inside debt and its role in managerial compensation. *The Journal of Finance* 62 (4): 1551–1588.
Terviö, M. 2008. The difference that CEOs make: An assignment model approach. *The American Economic Review* 98 (3): 642–668.
Thanassoulis, J.E. 2012. The case for intervening in Bankers' Pay. *Journal of Finance* 67 (3): 849–895.
Thanassoulis, J., and M. Tanaka. 2018. Optimal pay regulation for too-big-to-fail banks. *Journal of Financial Intermediation* 33: 83–97.
Vallascas, F., and J. Hagendorff. 2013. CEO bonus compensation and bank default risk: Evidence from the US and Europe. *Financial Markets, Institutions & Instruments* 22 (2): 47–89.
Zalewska, A. 2016. A new look at regulating bankers' remuneration. *Corporate Governance: An International Review* 24 (3): 322–333.

Chapter 4
Characteristics and Pay Packages of CEOs at the Largest European Banks: Some Empirical Evidence

Abstract Do the personal and professional characteristics of CEOs play a role in the performance and risk-exposure of the largest European financial conglomerates? Are their compensation structures alike? In this chapter, we empirically test these relationships, highlighting the main differences with the results reported in the literature and addressing future research directions. We present descriptive statistics of our sample of financial conglomerates and related CEOs before presenting our empirical evidence. We construct two models: one where the dependent variable is Tobin's q, as a proxy for conglomerate performance, and the other where the dependent variable is the financial conglomerate risk. Since financial conglomerates have complex and diversified businesses, we construct the model from an income and asset diversity perspective. Our first analysis shows that CEO tenure and experience in the financial industry are factors that enhance the market value of financial conglomerates, although having an older CEO might be detrimental. Moreover, while bonuses have positive effects on performance, the fixed components of CEO remuneration are value-destroying. On the one hand, professional experience typically helps a CEO to achieve higher performance; on the other, it increases a bank's risk exposure. Tenure length, however, could act as a hedging mechanism.

4.1 Introduction

As outlined in Chap. 3, the relationship between executive compensation and risk-taking varies systematically across banks and depends on several factors. DeYoung et al. (2013) and Thanassoulis and Tanaka (2018) point out that this relation is less evident for very large banks. In fact, very large banks have extensive experience in providing highly aggressive risk-taking incentives, have the strongest growth opportunities, and can exploit their TBTF status. In the case of TBTF, when CEOs are compensated through debt-like measures (inside debt), the debt part fails to mitigate project choice distortion when debt markets are informed. Moreover, while at most banks the board of directors reduce CEO vegas in order to discourage undesirable levels of risk-taking, for very large banks, boards instead reinforce risk-taking by holding steady or even increasing CEO vegas. Most studies have dealt with US

C. Curi and M. Murgia, *Bank CEOs*, SpringerBriefs in Finance,
https://doi.org/10.1007/978-3-319-90866-3_4

banks and only a handful have considered EU banks. However, none of them has analysed this issue in financial conglomerates. Financial conglomerates are diversified, large, complex institutions that provide, under a single corporate entity, commercial banking, securities underwriting and trading, asset management, insurance and other nonbank financial activities.[1] These behemoths control hundreds of operating subsidiaries and affiliates in foreign markets and manage investments in nonfinancial sectors. The trend in the conglomeration of financial institutions has increased remarkably worldwide during recent decades, with an increasing proportion of assets held by conglomerates and more widespread offers of financial services (Carmassi and Herring 2012). Among bankers, regulators, policymakers and economists, there is an intense debate on the activities, efficiency and huge sizes that these institutions have reached in recent times (Boot 2011; Saunders and Walter 2012; Admati and Hellwig 2014). One consequence of these very large banks is the threat they pose to the financial stability of the banking sector and the economic sector in general. It follows that the CEOs leading this type of bank might look like "superstars", as first proposed in Rosen's (1981) seminal paper.

We might observe diverse characteristics in the CEOs running such financial conglomerates. Financial conglomerates are corporate structures that offer various financial products and services in retail banking, insurance, asset management, lending to nonfinancial businesses, investment banking and housing finance "under one roof" (referred to as a universal banking model). Hence, they might need to be managed by a generalist CEO rather than a specialist one. Moreover, it is well known that financial conglomerates' market values are typically discounted with respect to the whole value of matched specialised financial institutions. Are CEOs in financial conglomerates specifically appointed to counter this natural discounting effect? If such a link could be established, we would expect to observe that the CEOs of large financial firms have skills in performing more complex tasks such as acquisitions and organisational restructuring, as Custódio et al. (2013) found for nonfinancial firms. Do CEO compensation packages include the right incentives to foster value-enhancing investments, divestments and other strategic changes? These questions make it relevant to investigate whether CEO characteristics such as age, education, tenure, past professional experience in the industry and pay structure have any effect on financial conglomerates' performance and risk exposure. Empirical evidence on this relationship is very scarce. This chapter aims to extend this area of research to the banking industry and its "superstar CEOs" by drawing on the vast theoretical and empirical literature which has, so far, mainly focused on nonfinancial firms.

[1] See Curi (2017) for a survey on the economics and market valuation of financial conglomerates.

4.2 Data, Sample Selection Criteria, and Variable Construction

Following prior studies on financial conglomerates and diversification discounting (Laeven and Levine 2007; Schmid and Walter 2009; Curi and Murgia 2018), we drew a sample from the Bankscope database. The sample was selected according to the following process:

1. Select financial firms (SIC 6000-6799), and exclude real estate firms (SIC 6500), savings, mutual, cooperative banks, and government-controlled credit institutions.
2. Retain only diversified financial institutions (based on both asset diversification and income diversification) and adopt the consensus of existing literature in defining what constitutes diversification (e.g. Laeven and Levine 2007). Asset-diversified financial conglomerates are considered banks with ratios of loans to total earning assets of between 10 and 90%. Income-diversified financial conglomerates are considered banks with ratios of gross interest revenue to total operating income of between 10 and 90%.
3. Select the 30 largest publicly-traded European financial institutions by total assets, as of year-end 2005.
4. Identify the financial conglomerates' CEOs.
5. Obtain data on CEO characteristics and compensation structures from different sources (e.g. LexisNexis, financial reports, Wikipedia).
6. Remove financial conglomerates with missing financial data.

The final dataset includes 24 European financial conglomerates that were analysed over the period 2005–2013, yielding a total of 216 bank-year observations. Table 4.1 shows the final sample of financial conglomerates, the countries of their headquarters, and their total assets as of year-end 2005. As Table 4.2 shows, France and UK had more than four financial conglomerates while other countries had between one and three. The striking picture that emerges is the high number of CEOs that exist in countries with relatively small numbers of financial conglomerates. This is the case in Belgium which, although having only two financial conglomerates, had eight CEOs at the helm in the 2005–2013 period. Italy is another interesting case where we uncovered a relatively high CEO turnover. The UK is a special case in our sample, as it is the country with the highest CEO turnover and number of financial conglomerates.

We used Tobin's q as a market-based performance measure and the standard deviation of profitability (SD_{ROA}) as a proxy for risk.[2] Moreover, following the most established empirical findings, we focus on four CEO characteristics that might affect financial conglomerate performance and risk. They are: (i) CEO age, (ii) length of CEO appointment (tenure), (iii) previous experience in the financial sector, and (iv) whether or not the CEO has a college degree. Moreover, we consider two components of the pay structure: (i) the fixed share and (ii) the bonus share. Since financial

[2]More complicated risk measures could be adopted (see references in Chap. 3).

Table 4.1 List of financial conglomerates in the sample

Financial conglomerate	Country	Total assets (€ bn 2013)
Barclays PLC	UK	1391
HSBC Holdings PLC	UK	1313
BNP Paribas	France	1297
ING Group NV	Netherlands	1195
Royal Bank of Scotland Group PLC (The)	UK	1169
Deutsche Bank AG	Germany	1023
Banco Santander SA	Spain	835
UniCredit SPA	Italy	812
Intesa Sanpaolo	Italy	551
Dexia	Belgium	524
Lloyds Banking Group PLC	UK	466
Commerzbank AG	Germany	458
Natixis	France	451
Banco Bilbao Vizcaya Argentaria SA	Spain	404
Royal Bank of Canada RBC	Canada	348
Danske Bank A/S	Denmark	336
KBC Group NV/KBC Group SA	Belgium	336
Nordea Bank AB (PUBL)	Sweden	336
Skandinaviska Enskilda Banken AB	Sweden	208
Credit Industriel et Commercial—CIC	France	202
Standard Chartered PLC	UK	188
Svenska Handelsbanken	Sweden	174
Bank of Ireland	Ireland	172
Banca Monte dei Paschi di Siena SPA	Italy	158

conglomerates are very large banks, we also control for their higher level of organisational complexity by inserting measures of size and degree of diversification.

Table 4.3 provides descriptive statistics of the financial conglomerates in our sample and their CEOs.

The mean CEO age was higher than that typically reported in other studies (e.g. Nguyen et al. 2015, which used a US bank sample), suggesting that large European banks employ older CEOs than US banks. Mean tenure was 6.55 years and less than half of the CEOs had previous experience in the financial industry. Most of them had a college degree. Looking at compensation structures, we found that fixed salary share

Table 4.2 Breakdown of financial conglomerates and CEOs by home country

Country	Financial conglomerates		CEO	
	Number	Percentage	Number	Percentage
Belgium	2	8	8	15
Denmark	1	4	3	6
France	4	17	7	13
Germany	2	8	4	7
Ireland	1	4	2	4
Italy	3	13	7	13
Netherland	1	4	3	6
Spain	2	8	3	6
Sweden	3	13	5	9
United Kingdom	5	21	12	22
Total	24	100%	54	100%

Table 4.3 Summary statistics of CEOs and financial conglomerates sampled in this study

	Nobs	Mean	SD
CEO characteristics			
Age (years)	216	54.77	7
Tenure (year)	216	6.55	4
Financial industry expertise (dummy variable)	209	0.14	0.36
College degree (dummy variable)	209	0.40	0.49
Compensation structure			
Fixed salary share	189	0.32	0.13
Bonus share	189	0.23	0.28
Total compensation (€ million)	189	3.53	3
Financial conglomerate characteristics			
Tobin's *q*	216	0.99	0.07
Risk (%)	216	0.40	0.29
Leverage	216	0.05	0.02
Total assets (€ billion)	216	697.60	576.51
Income diversity	216	0.47	0.20
Asset diversity	216	0.74	0.17
Interests/total operating income	216	0.39	0.19
Loans/total earning assets	216	0.51	0.16

is higher than the bonus share. Moreover, the bonus share is slightly lower compared to the findings in Vallascas and Hagendorff (2013). This difference might be due to different time periods under investigation, as we include also the sovereign financial crisis. Financial conglomerates' average market valuations were on par with those of similar studies, and our sample seemed less risky although much larger in terms of total assets than those of similar studies (e.g. Bai and Elyasiani 2013). The income and asset diversity indices were computed as in Laeven and Levine (2007), and indicate that the financial conglomerates in our sample were diversified more under the asset-based perspective than the income-based prospective. That is further confirmed by looking at a balanced distribution between assets (loans vs other earning assets), given that the ratio of loans to total earning assets equals 51%. The lower value of the interest to total operating income ratio suggests that these financial conglomerates are more focused on non-lending activities and, therefore, activities related to asset management, trading and insurance, etc. Overall, our analyses investigate the impacts of the characteristics and remuneration packages of CEOs managing very large financial intermediaries on performance and risk.

4.3 Results and Discussion

The following empirical analyses aim to assess the relationship between financial conglomerate performance (and risk) and CEO characteristics and compensation structures. It also aims to control for other relevant factors such as complexity, size and diversity, which could also play significant roles in financial conglomerate performance and risk outcomes. Our econometric approach employs standard Ordinary Least Squares regression models that control for unobserved variables that are constant over time through annual fixed effects. Further, since individual financial conglomerate observations are clearly not independent, we computed cluster-robust standard errors and treated each financial conglomerate as a cluster. The set of explanatory variables were lagged at time $t - 1$ in order to minimise possible endogeneity issues. Regression variables included tenure, total compensation and total assets computed in logarithm form. Moreover, as diversification and business orientation could be valued from the income and asset perspectives, we estimated pooled time-series cross-sectional regressions from the income perspective (Table 4.4, columns 1 and 2) and asset perspective (Table 4.4, columns 3 and 4), inserting, alternatively, the diversity index or the business orientation index.

We first constructed two models. *Model 1*, reported in Panel A Table 4.4, uses the dependent variable of the conglomerate performance metric Tobin's q, while *Model 2*, reported in Panel B Table 4.4, uses the dependent variable of SD_{ROA}, which is a proxy for conglomerate level of risk.

As expected, CEO characteristics were influential. The coefficient of age was negative and significant under both perspectives. This indicates that financial conglomerates managed by older CEOs could suffer inefficiency that translates as performance loss. On the other hand, both tenure and financial industry experience

Table 4.4 Multivariate analysis

Panel A: Model 1—dependent variable Tobin's q

	Income-based		Asset-based	
	(1)	(2)	(3)	(4)
Age	−0.093*	−0.104**	−0.109**	−0.089*
	(−1.930)	(−2.168)	(−2.281)	(−1.945)
Tenure	0.019*	0.016	0.014	0.019*
	(1.866)	(1.600)	(1.475)	(1.865)
Financial industry experience	0.034**	0.040***	0.032**	0.034**
	(2.332)	(2.912)	(2.274)	(2.469)
College degree	0.012	0.009	0.010	0.017
	(1.079)	(0.788)	(0.943)	(1.436)
Fixed salary share	−0.022***	−0.018***	−0.018***	−0.021***
	(−4.230)	(−3.395)	(−3.502)	(−4.033)
Bonus share	0.027***	0.026***	0.026***	0.028***
	(4.912)	(4.392)	(4.484)	(4.765)
Total compensation	0.037***	0.041***	0.040***	0.042***
	(6.806)	(8.134)	(7.488)	(8.288)
Leverage	1.109***	0.814**	1.153***	1.245***
	(2.924)	(2.042)	(2.973)	(3.456)
Total assets	−0.022***	−0.013*	−0.014**	−0.025***
	(−2.653)	(−1.897)	(−2.083)	(−2.937)
Income diversity	0.067*			
	(1.957)			
Interests/total operating income		0.060		
		(1.049)		
Asset diversity			−0.046	
			(−1.426)	
Loans/total earning assets				−0.090**
				(−2.283)
Constant	1.239***	1.189***	1.279***	1.334***
	(6.306)	(6.142)	(6.037)	(6.208)
Observations	161	165	165	165
R-squared	0.513	0.488	0.492	0.499
Year FE	Yes	Yes	Yes	Yes

(continued)

Table 4.4 (continued)

Panel B: Model 2—dependent variable SD_{ROA}				
	Income-based		Asset-based	
	(1)	(2)	(3)	(4)
Age	−0.002	0.001	0.001	−0.000
	(−0.965)	(0.521)	(0.636)	(−0.195)
Tenure	−0.001***	−0.001***	−0.001***	−0.001***
	(−3.266)	(−3.000)	(−2.810)	(−3.555)
Financial industry experience	0.002**	0.002***	0.003***	0.003***
	(2.193)	(2.719)	(3.078)	(3.626)
College degree	0.000	0.001	0.001	0.000
	(1.156)	(1.451)	(1.310)	(0.035)
Fixed salary share	−0.001**	−0.001***	−0.001***	−0.001***
	(−2.473)	(−3.408)	(−3.480)	(−2.640)
Bonus share	0.001**	0.001**	0.001**	0.001**
	(2.074)	(2.541)	(2.537)	(2.052)
Total compensation	−0.000	−0.001**	−0.001**	−0.001***
	(−1.367)	(−2.485)	(−2.142)	(−2.693)
Leverage	0.045***	0.028	0.017	0.003
	(2.860)	(1.425)	(0.875)	(0.187)
Total assets	0.000	−0.001**	−0.001*	0.000
	(1.364)	(−2.090)	(−1.900)	(1.205)
Income diversity	−0.006***			
	(−4.756)			
Interests/total operating income		−0.002		
		(−0.795)		
Asset diversity			0.001	
			(1.111)	
Loans/total earning assets				0.008***
				(4.341)
Constant	0.011	0.014*	0.011	0.003
	(1.503)	(1.689)	(1.370)	(0.402)
Observations	161	165	165	165
R-squared	0.374	0.289	0.292	0.374
Year FE	Yes	Yes	Yes	Yes

*Significant at 10%, ** significant at 5%, and *** significant at 1%

played positive roles. This implies that financial industry CEOs that have been within the same firm and industry for longer have better abilities in managing complex institutions, making sophisticated decisions and carrying out restructuring programs than CEOs with less tenure and experience. This evidence might also be related to the positive effects that social networks might generate when working in the same environment. Lastly, education had no influence on bank performance.

When we look at compensation structures, our results confirm the results found in King et al. (2016) with respect to the positive effect of cash compensation, namely, bonuses. However, we also found that the level of fixed salary had a negative effect on financial conglomerate performance. The total compensation measure also has a positive effect on financial conglomerate performance, confirming previous papers that have discussed the striking increases in CEO compensation and their effects on performance. Controls for financial conglomerate characteristics enter with expected sign, in particular, variables that are related to leverage, size and income diversification.

In Panel B Table 4.4, only the variable that measures financial industry experience retains the same sign as in Panel A, while age turns to be insignificant, and tenure switches to a negative and statistically significant estimate. Hence, while tenure length correlates with a lower level of conglomerate risk, higher CEO experience in the financial industry is likely to increase conglomerate risk. It is plausible to assume that a CEO with more expertise feels more confident in undertaking risky investment strategies and ends up increasing conglomerate risk. In contrast to Vallascas and Hagendorff (2013), we reveal that higher bonuses are correlated with higher bank risk, although with a small magnitude. Also in *Model 2*, controls for leverage, size and the income diversification of financial conglomerates enter with expected sign.

Summing up, our empirical results indicate that CEOs' personal and professional characteristics have significant influences on financial conglomerate performance and risk. Nonetheless, their impacts are opposing, given that higher risk might give higher performance. This research area needs to be further investigated, as there are still unanswered questions in this field. Extending the analysis to the entire spectrum of Global Systemic Important Banks (G-SIBs), and analysing the relationship between large conglomerate TBTF status and CEO characteristics would be a fruitful avenue of research. Moreover, as our study shows conflicting results in the relationship between compensation structure and bank risk, a more sophisticated approach is necessary to examine this important link, as well as a better sample that contains a richer set of CEO personal and professional characteristics.

References

Admati, A., and M. Hellwig. 2014. *The Bankers' New Clothes: What's Wrong With Banking and What to do About it*. Princeton University Press.

Bai, G., and E. Elyasiani. 2013. Bank stability and managerial compensation. *Journal of Banking & Finance* 37 (3): 799–813.

Boot, A.W. 2011. Banking at the crossroads: How to deal with marketability and complexity? *Review of Development Finance* 1 (3): 167–183.

Carmassi, J., and R. Herring. 2012. The corporate structure of international financial conglomerates: Complexity and its implications for safety and soundness. In *The Oxford Handbook of Banking*, ed. A. Berger, Molyneux, P., and Wilson, J. Oxford: Oxford University Press.

Curi, C. 2017. *Valuing Financial Conglomerates: Stylised Factors and New Evidence from Financial Crises*. FrancoAngeli.

Curi, C., and M. Murgia. 2018. Divestitures and financial conglomerate excess value. *Journal of Financial Stability* 36: 187–207.

Custódio, C., M.A. Ferreira, and P. Matos. 2013. Generalists versus specialists: Lifetime work experience and chief executive officer pay. *Journal of Financial Economics* 108 (2): 471–492.

DeYoung, R., E.Y. Peng, and M. Yan. 2013. Executive compensation and business policy choices at U.S. Commercial Banks. *Journal of Financial and Quantitative Analysis* 48 (1): 165–196.

King, T., A. Srivastav, and J. Williams. 2016. What's in an education? Implications of CEO education for bank performance. *Journal of Corporate Finance* 37: 287–308.

Laeven, L., and R. Levine. 2007. Is there a diversification discount in financial conglomerates? *Journal of Financial Economics* 85 (2): 331–367.

Nguyen, D.D.L., J. Hagendorff, and A. Eshraghi. 2015. Which executive characteristics create value in banking? Evidence from appointment announcements. *Corporate Governance: An International Review* 23 (2): 112–128.

Rosen, S. 1981. The Economics of Superstars. *American Economic Review* 71: 845–858.

Saunders, A., and I. Walter. 2012. Financial architecture, systemic risk, and universal banking. *Financial Markets and Portfolio Management* 26 (1): 39–59.

Schmid, M.M., and I. Walter. 2009. Do financial conglomerates create or destroy economic value? *Journal of Financial Intermediation* 18 (2): 193–216.

Thanassoulis, J., and M. Tanaka. 2018. Optimal pay regulation for too-big-to-fail banks. *Journal of Financial Intermediation* 33: 83–97.

Vallascas, F., and J. Hagendorff. 2013. CEO bonus compensation and bank default risk: Evidence from the US and Europe. *Financial Markets, Institutions & Instruments* 22 (2): 47–89.

Chapter 5
Conclusions

Abstract This concluding chapter offers our view on the challenges that bank CEOs will have to address in the near future. The extensive transformations that will overwhelm the banking industry in the years to come will test even the most talented CEO. Those transformations will extend from accepting and investing in the revolutionary technologies that will be part of future banking business models, to design strategic decisions in a fierce and competitive financial sector and at the same time complying with an increasing difficult financial system regulatory framework. At the end, in the way CEOs are recruited, incentivised, retained and compensated will be one of most crucial decision banks have to take to succeed in a competitive, complex and integrated global financial system.

Bank CEOs' characteristics and compensation contracts will stay high on the research agenda in the near future, given the extensive transformations of business models and advent of new technologies and regulatory frameworks that will shape the banking industry. In the years to come, banks will be challenged to invest massively in digitisation if they want to retain their franchises and improve customer experiences, revenues and efficiency. However, advances in technology and changing customer experiences might lead to the emergence of an integrated-network economy where traditional personal customer relationships might be threatened. To improve the major drivers of performance, such as revenue growth, cost efficiency, operational effectiveness and customer satisfaction, banks must embark on an ambitious transformation that affects all aspects of their businesses. Needless to say, bank CEOs will have the difficult role of simultaneously being the "bank horse" and "bank jockey". In turn, bank performance will mostly depend on the specific CEO appointed to a specific bank. Not all CEOs currently possess the capabilities, skills and culture they need to operate in challenging times that may require specific attitudes and talents. In this landscape, bank CEOs will come under scrutiny from many constituents: shareholders, bondholders, depositors, employees, academics, policymakers and industry experts.

This book analysed different aspects of bank CEOs' personal and professional characteristics, and the peculiar traits of their compensation packages, which is unquestionably one of the most discussed topics in the current banking sector.

C. Curi and M. Murgia, *Bank CEOs*, SpringerBriefs in Finance,
https://doi.org/10.1007/978-3-319-90866-3_5

Although much is known about their compensation structures, a lot remains to be understood about the influence of biographical characteristics. Moreover, these questions are even less well known in relation to European banks, which are characterised by greater heterogeneity in their CEO profiles due to international differences in culture, regulations and banking systems. We have highlighted that some CEO characteristics affect bank performance more than others. Moreover, given the same characteristics, the effects on performance and risk could be opposing. How can we reconcile this apparent conflict? We further analysed how risk-taking incentives embedded in CEO contracts might distort their investment policies and other strategic decisions, but failed to reach a clear conclusion. Differences emerged when comparing US and European banks, and very large banks and small banks. Regulatory interventions have created even larger distortions, exacerbating excessive risk-taking behaviour. Although the executive compensation literature and the understanding of CEO pay practices have grown, many questions remain unanswered. Further research questions might ask whether bank CEO characteristics should change in the near future, and how? Moreover, should pay contracts be mostly embedded with equity-like or debt-like components to provide the best outcome for all parties? Are very large banks subject to the same optimally constrained compensation structure? What are the right incentives to motivate CEOs to adapt to the disruptive innovations that will swamp banks in years to come?

Further research is essential in order to contribute to the debate on the effects of CEO characteristics and compensation structures on bank performance.

FSC
www.fsc.org
MIX
Papier | Fördert gute Waldnutzung
FSC® C083411

Kolibri 360 GmbH
Ferdinand-Jühlke-Straße 7
99095 Erfurt, Deutschland
produktsicherheit@kolibri360.de